Airb

CW00496149

Soldier

from RASC Air Despatcher to the SAS

By Brian (Harry) Clacy

Dedication

This book is dedicated to W/427492 Pte E Dower WRAC, 6 Training Regt, Yeovil. Eunice served in the WRAC and she eventually chaperoned a Cpl Terry Byrne RCT in the NAAFI bar at Lufton Camp, Yeovil.

1st April 1948 – 18th July 2023

The following is an excerpt from my book 'Soldiers on Wheels' which tells the story of how Eunice Dower met Terry Byrne.

'Terry's B1 Course was held in Lufton Camp, which co-incidentally was where the Women's Royal Army Corps (WRAC) accommodation was located. The men's accommodation was positioned in Houndstone Camp, Yeovil on the other side of a road, surrounded by tall security fences. Male soldiers were only allowed admission into Lufton Camp for the duration of their Course lessons and if they were signed into the camp by a female soldier during the evenings (WRAC soldiers were only allowed to sign in one male soldier each), all male soldiers were strictly forbidden from entering the female accommodation at any time. If a soldier was lucky enough to get an evening invite into the NAAFI Club by a Women's Royal Army Corps (WRAC) soldier, he had to be accompanied by that young

lady at all times and escorted back to the guardroom to be signed back out again by 2200 hours, and not a minute later.

Terry didn't have a WRAC girlfriend whilst on his B1 Course, so there was no way he could get into the NAAFI Bar for a few quiet beers in the evening. This is where a petit 19-year-old WRAC Clerk called Private Eunice Dower comes into the picture. Eunice had a WRAC friend called Sue who asked Eunice, "Can I book a soldier into camp using your name, he's a mate of my boyfriend and he only wants to get into the NAAFI Bar for a few quiet beers." Eunice originally came from Abercynon in South Wales and regardless of her diminutive stature; she could be a formidable person when annoyed. As a special favour to Sue, Eunice signed Cpl Terry Byrne RCT (Sue's boyfriends' mate) into the camp and then watched him saunter off into the NAAFI bar. Like all good RCT soldiers, he was chasing down the scent of proper ale. By 2200 hours Terry hadn't returned to the guardroom so Eunice could account for him and sign him back out of Lufton Camp. A slightly miffed Private Eunice Dower WRAC boldly marched into the NAAFI Bar and started shouting, "Corporal Byrne! Corporal Byrne! Come on Corporal Byrne, you should've been out of here by now, get yourself down to the Guardroom immediately, you need to be signed out of the camp! NOW!"

That incident set a precedent for Eunice for the next 50 years, because Terry and Eunice were married in her home town in South Wales on 15th June 1968, and she's been hollering at him ever since!'

Eunice was as much a dedicated soldier as her husband Terry and George Henderson.

Preface

This Book is to commemorate all the soldiers who served in the Royal Army Service Corps (RASC), the Royal Corps of Transport (RCT), and the Royal Logistic Corps (RLC), before going on to serve in the Special Air Service (SAS).

Brigadier Andrew Massey

Lieutenant Colonel Sam Mallett

Ken Borthwick

John Tidewell

Kenny Searle

Geordie Nicholas

Andy Wheeler

George Henderson

The above listed are just a few of those who not only passed SAS 'Selection', but who also achieved the ultimate accolade by qualifying as HGV Trog Drivers before joining 63 (Para) Sqn RCT, (63 Parachute Squadron RCT).

<u>Quote</u>

"I did my job as a soldier.
I've done everything that was asked of me."

**Major George Henderson MBE
(RASC, RCT, RLC and SAS Ret'd)**

CHAPTERS

Acknowledgements

This book couldn't have been written by me on my lonesome, there are so many people I have to thank for some desperately needed help.

The first I have to mention is obviously George Henderson. He has done so much and worked very hard on the details of this book. He has also had to endure many hours of talking to the author on zoom and battled through an old but still reoccurring illness from his days serving overseas with the SAS.

Secondly, it's got to be my wife Nicky, she has also worked so very hard; you can't imagine what she's done and the hours she's put in to get this book finished for you all to read. She's also nursed me through all the stages of my illness, Hydrocephalus, and continues to do so. Thank you darling, there aren't enough words in the Oxford English Dictionary to fully explain my love and admiration for you.

Added to this I have to mention Driver Steve Drew RCT who served in 35 Sqn RCT at Duisburg under the command of WO2 (SSM) George Henderson RCT. By the way, Steve is the person who initiated the writing of this book - you're a top geezer Steve.

Major (Retired) Terry Cavender, has read and corrected every sentence of this book as it has been written. Tel, your advice, help and support to my wife Nicky and I has been unparalleled, we cannot thank you enough.

To everyone who has read even one of my books, I would I like to thank you all for your support and encouragement. Greatly appreciated.

CHAPTER ONE

BASIC TRAINING

515817 Major George Henderson MBE
RASC, RCT and SAS

George Henderson was born in Haddo House, Aberdeen in 1944. This Scottish Stately Home, belonging to Lord Aberdeen, was an emergency Maternity Hospital for mothers who had been evacuated from the City of Glasgow because of the German Luftwaffe bombing of the City. About 1,200 Haddo babies were born in 'Haddo' during World War Two (WW2). Bizarrely, a week after George had been safely delivered he and his mother returned to the dangers of being bombed in Glasgow.

George's dad, Thomas Rankin Henderson, was an RAF Airframe Fitter who served out in India during WW2. Like many Servicemen and Women, he never saw a shot fired in anger during the war. He had, however, helped to keep the RAF's Air-freighters and Hurricane fighters fully serviceable and in flying condition. Hurricane fighters were mainly used for reconnaissance (recce) missions because there was a real lack of need for an offensive/defensive Air Force in India during WW2. The Imperial Japanese Forces barely scratched the surface of India when they invaded from Burma, (now Myanmar). The majority of the country remained untainted, apart from Imphal and Kohima on the eastern side of India, both of which were not far from the Indian and Burmese borders.

'Aircraftsman Thomas Henderson and Elizabeth Pearl Crichton on their wedding day.'

When George's dad was released from his wartime service he worked as a Civilian Ambulance Driver for what became part of the modern-day National Health Service (NHS) in 1946 -1948.

George Henderson and his Mum's midwife from 1944 in Haddo House, she was still working there as a midwife in the 1980s

After the war, living accommodation in the city of Glasgow was so scarce that the Henderson family initially moved into George's maternal grandparents house at 29 Shawbridge Street, Pollokshaws.

At that time, Pollokshaws was a borough, which later was incorporated as a district of the city of Glasgow. In 1947 a rental apartment in a tenement at 44 Wemyss Street, Cowcaddens very near to the city centre became vacant and made available to the Henderson family. It was a very old building and George remembers seeing gas-light sconces on the walls of the rooms, which gives a good indication of the age of the run-down building.

There was no running hot water in the apartment, just a cold water tap at the kitchen sink. Bath nights were in a tin bath in front of a coal fire and the bath had to be filled via boiled kettles. The water in the bath was never more than 3 or 4 inches deep, but that was enough for the small boys. There was no internal toilet, instead the 'Cludgies' (Glasgow term for toilets) were on the stair-head landing and shared with the other two families on their floor. Every family had a key for the door and they locked it when inside in case someone tried to enter.

As the flats were most usually occupied with very low-income families, the luxury of toilet paper was not a high priority on shopping lists. Instead, good use was made of the previous day's 'Daily Record' newspaper, which was cut into squares with a piece of string threaded through a hole pierced in one of the corners, then hung on a nail on the inside of the cludgie door. Working on the premise that, "The job wasnae finished until the paperwork was done," those who had invested in proper toilet paper took it with them into the toilet, then returned with the unused segment of the roll back to their accommodation.

If, when going up or down the stairs in the mornings, you met someone from one of the other flats who was carrying a large object covered in a cloth, you averted your eyes as they were more than likely disposing of the previous night's body effluence, which was contained in a 'potty.'

A lot of fun was had playing along with other kids who lived in the street and its surrounds, particularly in the deserted 'dunnies' (dungeons/cellars), a series of empty, darkened rooms below the ground floor flats that were used for some purpose by the building occupants from an earlier era. The damp musty smell that pervaded throughout the dunnies remains in George's memory banks to this very day! Kids never ventured into them after dark as it was the territory of the 'Bogey' Men.

George had one older and one younger brother. John was born in 1943 and went on to become a Mechanical Engineer. His younger brother, Colin, was born in 1947 and he became an Electrical Engineer.

During the 'Glasgow Fair,' (a Glasgow traditional holiday fortnight), the city virtually closed down and emptied as families went on holiday. This was in the days well before affordable foreign package holidays and flights to popular places abroad. Blackpool was very popular, as were other seaside resorts. The Henderson's though, went to the countryside and stayed in a farmhouse near Balfron, a few miles north of Glasgow for their holidays.

**George with his Mum
and younger brother, Colin**

**George at Dunnard Street School, Maryhill,
Glasgow, 6th from left rear rank**

Whilst there, George used to help the owner of the cottage, the farmer, herd his cows from the fields into the byre (a Scottish cow shed) then watched the milking process and later he helped get the cattle back to the fields.

This spiked an interest for George and from it, he decided he wanted to work on a farm, with the ultimate intention of becoming a Farm Manager when he was old enough to work for a living.

To that end, Glasgow Corporation had obtained two farms that they turned into an Agricultural School (Lawmuir). The joining age to attend the school was fourteen years but at the age of thirteen and a half, George applied for one of the vacancies to attend there as a student and was accepted. He and the other young lads would continue with their academic studies but also learned about animal husbandry. In addition to doing practical farm work, which included working with, and feeding farm animals such as cows, pigs, sheep and poultry. They were also taught about crop and field rotation theory. (*Author's Note*): *After the war, a lot of the families were drawn from farm work into city-life; the nation was moving away from the poorly paid rural jobs*).

When George was almost at the end of his studies at Lawmuir, a Balfron farmer approached the College to enquire if any of the students there would be interested in working for him. George met him for a discussion, after which it seemed to George a good idea at the time, as he needed to get some practical experience of what it would be like to work on a small farm, whilst at the same time the farmer would get someone with an idea of what farm work was really like.

Unfortunately, after 2 years of toil, George became fed up with the long hours and days of hard-work, and for a pittance of a wage. Whatever money George did receive was spent on extra warm clothing because in those days no-one was issued with Personal Protective Equipment (PPE). Farm workers had to provide their own weatherproof clothing to keep warm and dry when out working in the fields. Life on the farm was a never ending and thankless grind and George eventually started getting more than a bit fed up with it as his chosen career, so he started thinking about leaving and what he would do after farming.

One day, another friend of George's, who was also working on another nearby farm, told him that he also wanted to leave the farming industry. He'd heard that there was a Corps in the British Army that taught soldiers to drive all sorts of vehicles and that after completing basic training there was a good chance of being sent overseas to serve in foreign countries. He said that the name of the Corps was the Royal Army Service Corps (RASC). A short time later his pal left his job and went off to join up.

Four months later, George received a letter from his friend saying that he was now a trained soldier and driver in the Army and he was waiting to be posted to Germany. He said that the training in the red-bricked Buller Barracks in Aldershot, Hampshire, was very tough with lots of being shouted at, but said it was worth it, as obtaining his driving licence had now set him up for life. Also, he was shortly going to enjoy being in a different country.

That did it for George, his mind was made up that he too was going to join up. So, in April 1962 he handed in his notice to the farmer and a week later went into Glasgow to the Army Recruiting Office on Sauchiehall Street. On arrival, after some lengthy form filling, he was interviewed by a retired Army Major.

On reflection, George wonders what the Major must have thought of him, because, as he explained, "As a recruit, I hadn't got a clue about the Army or what they did. All my information came from war comics about the 'Loamshire Regiment' and the 'Red Devils' (Paras), who'd fought so fiercely against the Germans and the Japanese."

During the interview, the Major mentioned that at times particular Corps or Regiments might be fully manned so didn't need any new recruits. The Major then asked him, "just in case the RASC is not recruiting, what would your second choice of Regiment be?" George gave an emphatic reply, "The Paras!"

The Major simply raised an eyebrow then asked, "And what would be your third choice if the Paras are not recruiting?" George replied, "The Infantry." At that time he had no idea of the name of any of the particular Infantry Regiments. His mindset was purely concentrating on joining the only Corps he knew, and wanted to join '**The Royal Army Service Corps.**'

Quebec/Buller Barracks, Bordon & Aldershot, Hampshire

George left the Recruiting Office and went home to tell his family the good news about him finishing with farming and joining the British Army. A couple of days later, a Rail Warrant arrived in the post. It also contained printed instructions on how to get from Glasgow Central Railway Station to Bentley Station, Hants, and from there he had to get to Quebec Barracks, Bordon.

On the 27th of April 1962, George made his epic journey, the furthest ever from Glasgow, and duly arriving at Quebec Barracks. The last part of his journey was in the back of a Bedford RL 3 Tonner that had been waiting at Bentley Railway Station for recruits to arrive. Thankfully, this transport was there, as Bentley was quite remote and getting to Bordon from there would have been quite a task, especially as there was no public transport service.

Quebec Barracks was a 'holding camp' for RASC recruits. On arrival, he and quite a few others went through the completion of administration, then the issue of uniforms and webbing procedures. The NCO's at Bordon taught the recruits how to look after their kit, in particular the science of applying 'Blanco' paste to their webbing equipment and how to clean the brass buckles on their belts and packs. They were also instructed on ensuring that their uniforms were properly pressed, and also, how to get rid of little bubbles/blisters on leather boot outers by the use of a candle and heated spoon. They were also taken through the basics of marching in a squad and reminded of the importance of shaving every day; this included those youngsters who did not have any facial hair growing.

George remembers the awful smell emanating from the cookhouse and his first ever meal-sitting. The presentation of fried fish and chips appalled him. It bore no comparison to the world class 'fish suppers' he'd often enjoyed in Glasgow. George knew, however, that he would have to accept many changes and adapt to this new life.

Army uniforms being what they were, the recruits assumed they were made to fit alien beings. This necessitated several return visits to the Clothing Store in an effort to convince the Clothing Storeman, (who clearly had a warped sense of humour), that the more important clothing items, i.e. trousers/shirts, he'd been issued with were either two sizes too big, or too small. On one particular visit to the Quartermaster's (QM's) store, George noticed a commissioned officer walking on the other side of a road and thought to himself, "I wonder if I should salute him?" He didn't, and as they passed each other George just nodded at him. The officer doubtlessly realising that George was obviously a gormless recruit who had yet to be taught how to pay military compliments, simply nodded back and continued on his way.

Once Bordon had assembled enough recruits to make a sizable Intake, they were taken by truck to Buller Barracks, Aldershot, to start their basic training course. After an hour travelling in the rear of a Bedford RL 3-ton truck, wearing their new issued uniforms, they arrived at 'B Block' in Buller Barracks. The recruits were then housed in a large red brick accommodation building. Each recruit was allocated a bedspace with a large grey locker stood beside it. They were now collectively known as, 'Intake 35.'

It was a real wake-up call for George and the other recruits. One of the Junior Non-Commissioned Officer's (JNCO's), treated the recruits as human beings, but the Officer and Non-Commissioned Officer's (NCO's) were overly severe with them.

LCpl Drake, however, a very experienced soldier, had a different approach. He was always patient and encouraging and on the occasions that the squad had been given a particularly hard time, he would say to them, "Listen, don't get down-hearted by their attitude towards you. When you get to a working unit everything will change and you won't have to put up with any of this sort of crap." He was absolutely correct about that

In the early 1960's the British Army thought that being good at foot drill and being shouted at was a brilliant start for the basis of 'constructing' an ideal soldier. Although foot drill and moving together in a smart body of men was important, nowadays the emphasis is more on team building and career training. At Buller Barracks there was never any sense of encouragement for anyone who was struggling with the basic training. George took on board what LCpl Drake had told him, but some of the others didn't and a few of them paid £,a princely sum in those days), to purchase their discharge from the Army.

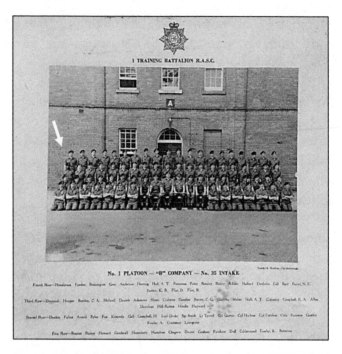

George's Basic Training Platoon. George is far left (see arrow) in the rear rank and LCpl Drake is in the 2nd Row sitting next to the Platoon Sgt.

George didn't know it at the time, but he could have claimed a free discharge because of his age. Had he known about that, or even if he'd had a spare £20 in his pocket, he freely admits that he would have considered hot footing it back to Glasgow.

At the beginning of the training, it had been agreed that each recruit would pay a small amount of money towards an 'End of training party.' With everybody contributing and the training nearing its end, thoughts started to turn towards the party night.

Unexpectedly, the recruit intake were told that the party was cancelled. When asked about the return of the contributions, the NCO's said that it would be paid into 'Pay Credits.' This is a feature of Army pay where underpayments and overpayments are adjusted accordingly.

Who would know any better The Corporals must, of course, be correct! However, an experienced Corporal who was re-enlisting and a member of the intake, Jack M, challenged the Troop NCO's by saying that paying into credits cannot be done. Identified, the NCO's then said that the money had 'gone missing.' As a result, no party and no refund on any money paid in.

In truth, George was quite relieved, as all he wanted to do was get training over with and move on to better Garrisons. He had found the basic training drill and 'bullshit' difficult but persevered and was determined to see this unpleasant phase through to the end. After all, he thought, countless others had done it and succeeded, including his friend Denis. On the flip side, he enjoyed weapons and fieldcraft training, so, at the end of the day it was all swings and roundabouts.

George had passed the basic training phase, (daily showering, cleaning teeth, marching, ironing his uniform etc). Driver Training on a Land Rover or a K9 truck should be next. Unexpectedly though, he became aware that an Officer was interviewing some of the recruits to confirm their chosen trade choice. At that time, in 1962, the RASC was responsible for training and providing the Army with Drivers, Cooks, Bakers, Butchers, Clerks and a few other trades.

George was sent for and was told by the Officer that he was not going to be a Driver, instead he was going to be put on a Clerks course. George had never written a letter in his life, the only things he'd ever put pen to paper on were Birthday and Christmas cards. He was shocked and wondered how he gave the impression that he could communicate on paper to other human beings. George's writing was undecipherable, the only person likely to understand it would possibly be a Doctor. After some persuasion, George convinced the now weary Officer that he did not want to be a Clerk. Alternatively, instead of a Military Transport (MT) pool George had heard about the RASC Air Despatch units, and it became his ambition to join them. The Officer accepted George's request and said that if he passed Driver Training then he would recommend him for Air Despatch (AD) Training.

CHAPTER TWO

AIR DESPATCH

6 Training Battalion RASC
Yeovil, Somerset

The next training phase was at the RASC Driver Training Battalion (6 Trg Bn RASC) at Houndstone Camp, just outside of Yeovil in Somerset.

On the square, in front of the Wooden 'Spider' accommodation blocks in Houndstone Camp, the intake of potential drivers met their new Platoon Commander, Lieutenant Spence RASC, who was a diminutive five foot tall, and their Platoon Sergeant, Sgt Parsons, who was a colossal six foot nine inches tall. Those two, and their rather long in the tooth, but very experienced Corporals, were the absolute antithesis of the Permanent Staff at Buller Barracks. Life at Yeovil was very relaxed and the military staff were extremely helpful and encouraging. The atmosphere away from the Aldershot basic training camp was so very different.

George was now starting to relax and enjoy his time in the Army. After the minimum hours of driver training, George passed his test in an Austin K9 Truck. There was only one fly in the ointment and that was on his driving test. The Examiner allocated to test George was rumoured to be the strictest soldier who had scored the most failures at Yeovil, and was the one person you didn't want as your Assessor. Anyway, he started out on the test and George felt that he was doing OK, but at a tricky left turn at a busy T junction in Swindon, George knew that he hadn't positioned his truck properly. He faced an instant failure on the test because he couldn't see the oncoming traffic coming from the right on the road he was about to join.

The approach to the junction was not a wide road, but what complicated the situation was a car parked incorrectly on the left just before the junction. As a result, George had to position his truck wider from the kerb which made it impossible to see approaching traffic from the right. In a 'light bulb' moment, George was saved because he looked across at the shop windows on the other side of the road and saw in the reflection a big enough gap to cross into the traffic coming from the right. He moved out safely, completed the turn and the remainder of the road test.

George had achieved his aim of passing his Driving Test. In addition, he felt that the Examiner did not deserve his labelled reputation because, from the start of the test, he was very helpful and had a very calming manner. George started to learn not to believe everything you're told as a Soldier, instead, work on the premise of never believing anything you were told!

55 (Air Despatch) Company RASC, Singapore

With all the basic training now finished, George confirmed his request to join the Air Despatch. A week later, he found himself at Watchfield Camp, a former RAF base just outside Swindon, which was also the RASC Air Despatch base.

Joining Air Despatch meant successfully attending a course where he and other students learned the basic methods of preparing and packing stores to be dropped by parachute from RAF Aircraft, (things like rations, water, ammunition and fuel). On completing the course, George travelled on an RAF Hastings Aircraft, (*Author's* Note): A*t one time these were the RAF's main Air-Transporters),* to RAF Lyneham; his first ever flight!

The course also involved learning about the different types of restraining cords and their breaking strains, vitally important as the cords were much used in the packing of stores that were dropped from aircraft. He learned how to prepare loads for air despatching and how to properly arrange and strap a vehicle to a Medium Stress Platform (MSP) before it was loaded into an RAF aircraft, which at that time was usually the huge Blackburn Beverley.

The seats in the Hastings were canvas and folded away on the side of the cabin. It was noisy, but not noticeable at the time, due to George's excitement. After take-off, he and the others were permitted to release seat belts and walk around the cabin. Mesmerised though, George spent most of the time looking out of the windows and remembers seeing part of the M1 under construction.

Air Despatch Wings
(Note - this set is an RASC pair, belonging to George Henderson).

In November 1962, the successful students assembled in a lecture room to learn of their postings to the various Air Despatch Units. The Course Officer said that he would call out locations and how many were needed for each of the Air Despatch units, which were based in Singapore, Aden, Kenya and home base (England). A show of hands was needed for whichever posting people preferred. Corporal Blake RASC had a course nominal roll and pencil at the ready. "OK, first off I want six volunteers for Sing..." George's hand shot up... "apore". Corporal Blake looked at George and ticked his sheet. The rest was a blur. When it was confirmed at the end of the posting brief and he was told that he was going to Singapore, he thought, "Is this really happening to me?"

A few days later, the six Air Despatchers who were being posted to 55 (AD) Coy RASC, Singapore were taken to RAF Lyneham in Wiltshire where they boarded an RAF Bristol Britannia, affectionately called, 'The Whispering Giant.' The nickname was due to the fact that the Britannia used the relatively new and quiet turbo prop engines, whereas the majority of ageing RAF propeller aircraft were still using the noisy piston engines.

After taking off on its long journey, the Britannia landed briefly in Germany, Cyprus, Aden and Istanbul, with passengers deplaning then emplaning at each stop. At each stop, cargo was being delivered and replaced from the hold. George will never forget when the aircraft doors were opened after landing at Aden and the blast of heat coming into the aircraft cabin which felt like someone had opened the doors of an oven. It shocked him.

George thought to himself, "How can people live in this sort of heat?" As he continued to gaze out of the aircraft's portal, he saw Royal Air Force (RAF) Airmen wearing shorts and Arabs in loose-fitting long white robes. In the distance he could see the visual distortion that shimmering heat from the tarmac was causing on distant objects, making them look like they were floating.

George would eventually find out what Aden was like to live in at a later period of his Army Career whilst serving during the British 'Climb Down' from their Aden Campaign.

Finally, the last leg of the journey to Singapore was from the tiny Indian Ocean island of Gan. Gan, an RAF base, was just another short stop for refuelling and offloading/loading of cargo. One passenger who joined the flight at RAF Gan looked like an Indian; he had very dark skin and was wearing an RAF tropical uniform (light khaki short sleeved shirt and shorts). When he boarded the aircraft he came and sat next to George. The plane took off and once again George looked out of the window watching the plane claw higher and higher into the clear blue sky

31

above the Indian Ocean. Suddenly and surprisingly, he heard, "Alright George, how you doing mate?" in a strong Glasgow accent. It was the 'Indian' Serviceman sat next to him.

Somewhat confused, George asked him how he knew his name. The Airman said, "It's me, George ... Tom. I lived in Dalmally Street, round the corner from you in Kirkland Street. We went to the same school together in Maryhill and were great friends." The penny dropped for George, his old friend Tom was so heavily suntanned that he'd looked like an Indian. Tom explained that after joining the RAF he'd been posted to RAF Gan and that he was on the 'plane because he was going to Singapore for some Rest & Recuperation (R&R). At that time RAF personnel, because of the isolation of Gan, were allowed to board any passing RAF aircraft if they had some time off. After arriving in Singapore, George never saw his old friend Tom again.

Arriving at RAF Changi Airport in Singapore on a wet and dark Sunday morning just after midnight, the aircraft doors were opened and the smell of jungle vegetation soon permeated throughout the plane. George was very familiar with this smell because he and his school friends often visited the Botanical Garden's green houses in Glasgow. The humidity, heat and smell was exactly the same.

After collecting their luggage, a soldier wearing a green tropical uniform approached them. On each shoulder of his shirt was sewn a 'flash' that showed a yellow Dakota emblem on a dark blue background, known as the 'Dakota Flash.'

The Dakota Flash originated as a Battle Honour worn by many Air Despatchers who'd flown at the Battle of Arnhem dropping vital supplies whilst under constant and heavy enemy fire on 'OPERATION MARKET GARDEN.' The loss of RAF Aircrew and Air Despatchers throughout was considerable.

'The Dakota Flash'
(Worn by the original Air Despatchers)

The Air Despatch driver told them to follow him to the transport, unsurprisingly a Bedford RL 3 Ton Truck. George managed to get a tailgate seat for the journey and as they drove out of RAF Changi Airport, he tried to take in everything he saw along the way, despite it being very dark.

It was difficult to see much because of the meagre street lights in the small villages but he could see lots of ram-shackled buildings, most of which had corrugated iron roofs. Many had empty stalls outside, indicating that when operating they were makeshift stores or shops, selling small goods or food. Later, he learned that they were perfect for passing travellers to stop off and buy tasty home-cooked snacks, cheap T-Shirts or even pairs of socks.

Eventually, the truck turned into and drove up a road into another village that would become extremely familiar to everyone. Again, there were empty market stalls on both sides of the street. Just beyond this street and village, called Jalan Kayu, was the entrance to the gates of RAF Seletar.

Jalan Kayu means 'Road Wood' in the Malayan language, and was most likely named after the person who planned the building of the base in 1937, (CE Wood). It was originally going to be called Air Base Road, but was called Jalan Kayu out of respect to the Malayan majority community.

Later, George, along with everyone else in RAF Seletar, would use the twice a week market outside the base to purchase many fast-moving items, like shirts, shorts, socks and flip flops. Some shops specialised in sending goods abroad, absolutely ideal for service people to send presents back home. George sent a magnificent tea service to his Mum. It was never used and has been passed back down to him, still unused. He wonders if he can get a refund if he takes it back to the shop!

At the end of the road the truck slowed to manoeuvre through gates manned by very smart RAF Policemen ('Snowdrops'). The white walls of the gate pillars and buildings inside, including the Guard Room, were very imposing. They had finally arrived at their destination, the camp, RAF Seletar, where 55 (AD) Coy RASC was based. The Air Despatch accommodation block was quite some distance from the Guardroom and the vehicle eventually pulled up and the driver switched its engine off outside a long three-storey white building surrounded by verandas on each of its floors.

George noticed that almost every double door was slatted and open and he could hear the sound of humming. This was coming from rotating ceiling fans in the rooms. He could also hear the noise of crickets and goodness knows what other creepy crawlies. George had heard these sounds before, but only in jungle war movies.

There was also the sound of a big bug buzzing around, it was much louder than the mosquitos (mossies). They were called a Cicada. The Air Despatchers had nicknamed them 'Beverley's' after the Blackburn Beverley, an RAF transport aircraft, because of their huge size. You were warned and quickly learned to watch out for these harmless insects, only because they could give you quite a shock if they crashed into you. In this case the Cicada hit a wall then fell to the ground; after a few seconds it started to walk around! These bugs only hatch every seventeen years, but they reach biblical plague levels before dying off again for another 17 years.

The Duty NCO emerged from one of the downstairs rooms and told the new arrivals to follow him to temporary accommodation where they could get their heads down. He told them they would be moved again once allocated to their particular Platoons that had their own segregated rooms in the block. They were told to report to the Company Sergeant Major (CSM) at Company Headquarters (Coy HQ) at 0900 hours on Monday morning.

After a restless couple of hours sleep, George and some of the others went to the Cookhouse for some breakfast, then did a recce around the huge camp and following various signposts, ended up at a very large and crowded swimming pool. George, being a red-headed and fair-skinned native of Scotland, was naturally prone to the usual sunburn in hot environments. (*Author's Note): Bet you didn't suffer much of that up in Scotland, George)?*

Later that afternoon, George got back to the accommodation and gradually felt his skin was getting very hot, red and painful, even though it had been a very overcast day. Unfortunately, he had become sunburnt, despite the cloud-cover. The rest of his night was spent sitting on a chair underneath a whirring fan, trying to get some cool comfort.

George loved hot sunny weather but he had quickly learned a new respect for it. It was something of which he would be forever wary about in later... pardon the pun... hotspots around the world. (*Author's Note: Sorry George).*

55 (AD) Coy RASC consisted of three Platoons (Plns); Iskander and Kemar that were at RAF Seletar, Singapore, and the third Carfax, which was based at the Royal Australian Air Force (RAAF) base in Butterworth, North West Malaya. George was posted to Iskander Pln, which was under the command of Lt Tony Case, assisted by Sgt Jack Robinson (troop members called him sailor - out of earshot - because he was an ex-merchant seaman).

Much of the work done at RAF Seletar was training. The Air Despatchers prepared practice packs, then loaded them onto either Blackburn Beverley's, De

Havilland Hastings or Twin Pioneer aircraft which were also based at RAF Seletar. The packs were despatched from the aircraft at various drop zones (DZs) around Singapore. Helicopter (Heli) handling and under-slinging loads were also practiced. The under-slung loads were ideal for getting supplies into jungle Dropping Zones, (DZs).

An important action of under-slinging is always to make sure that a 'ground spike' is used. Helicopters attract and hold static electricity whilst flying, and this electricity must be discharged to Earth before the aircraft hook is touched by anyone standing on the ground. Surplus and untamed electrical power could seriously injure or kill a person, as it uses the human body to earth all that power. So, 'Grounding' or 'Earth-spikes' were used to discharge static electricity from the Heli. The spikes are simply a length of heavy insulated wire with a metal spike at both ends. A section of these spikes were also insulated. Holding a spike by the insulated part, the other spike was pushed into the ground and the held spike was touched to the hook underneath the Heli, thereby discharging the static electricity to 'Earth' via the wire. As far as George ever knew, no one in 55 (AD) Coy RASC was ever 'shocked' by touching the hook from a helicopter before it had the static released, probably due to the thorough training that the Company went through.

There was, however, one particular faux pas that occurred whilst George was at 55 (AD) Coy RASC, although he wasn't in station at the time. The Commanding Officer (CO) had a pristine new Land Rover that was borrowed by the Air Despatchers for a Helicopter training exercise, practicing under-slinging. Unfortunately, after the vehicle had been hooked up and the Helicopter had taken off, the vehicle had separated from the aircraft in flight and it fell into the waters of the very deep Johore Straight at the end of the runway. No comments were ever recorded from the CO (none that were printable anyway!) and no one ever had the courage to suggest using the COs Land Rover for Helicopter drills again.

To give realistic training for the Air Despatchers and the RAF air crews, arrangements were made for an urn of tea and haversack rations (nosebags) to be issued from the cookhouse for the troops. This was followed by a drive across the causeway, that joined Singapore to Malaya, then a fifty-mile journey north to Batu Pahat. This is an open flat area used as a Drop Zone (DZ) for practice drop runs.

On arrival at the DZ, the ground crew laid out yellow panels in the form of a 'T' in the middle of the DZ for recognition by aircraft pilots to see. This was also the pilot's cue to commence the drops. Unfortunately, 'Ground to Air' Radios were not available for DZ teams in the early 1960's, so they did not have any voice communication with the aircraft pilots. It was simply a waiting game and a matter of keeping an ear open for the sound of four Bristol Centaur Aircraft engines approaching.

If there was a problem on the ground, this was conveyed to the pilots by adjusting the 'T' formation to indicate either a delay of the drop or cancellation. Most drops, however, were done within minutes of schedule and George, having done numerous DZ parties, never had a serious delay or cancellation.

Something puzzled George on those exercises though. How, he'd wondered, could a swarm of local Malayan villagers arrive at the DZ from the surrounding jungle by bicycle, and on foot, just before the sound of the aircraft engines heralded the arrival of an RAF aircraft delivery. How did they know? Jungle drums perhaps?

A familiar feature of life in South East Asia was the phenomenon of the 'Magnolia Man,' usually a local Malay, Chinese or Indian civilian sat astride a 50cc Honda motorbike with an ice bucket on the back. Soon after arrival, and setting up the DZ, these Far Eastern entrepreneurs would announce their arrival by ringing a school bell as they rode majestically towards the Air Despatchers.

Even when actually training in the 'Ulu' (Malay for jungle), those guys would appear on their motorcycles or bicycle with an ice box on the rear of it, ringing their bells and shouting "Magnolia!" (the brand name of the ice cream and lollies). When training in a hot steamy rainforest it was a welcome treat to have those entrepreneurs find you; they deserved a couple of extra dollars in exchange for their iced lollies, which helped to quench the constant thirst of working in the oppressive heat of the jungle.

The British Army's alternative to a 'Magnolia' thirst quencher will be familiar to all soldiers who have served in hot environments – i.e. the ration pack lemon or orange dry powder mixes which also hit the spot and was often referred to as 'Jungle Juice.' They were reputed to be so strong that they burnt holes in the lining of the average squaddies stomach. If true, then George's gut would now be like a sieve!

The same was rumoured about the ferocious curries (Kemah) served in 'Pop's' a canteen in Jalan Kayu!

The following photograph was taken whilst doing a resupply drop from an RAF Vickers Valletta Aircraft (Registration Number 156) when they were despatching supplies along the Thai/Malay Border. This aircraft was powered by twin Bristol Hercules 230 14 Cylinder radial engines. At the time George was established in the Royal Australian Air Force Base (RAAF) at Butterworth in North Malaya.

41

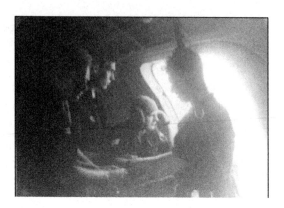

Left - right: Lance Corporal Dougie Lamb, Driver Lofty Robinson, Corporal Jack Warner (RASC) who was the Crew Commander, and Driver George Henderson

Cpl Jack Warner RASC, who is wearing the headset, talked to either the Pilot or the Navigator and he received the information from them when the plane was on a drop run and approaching the DZ. Cpl Jack Warner would instruct his AD team to prepare the packs for despatching and place them in the doorway with the parachute opening strops connected to strong points on the floor of the aircraft. They then await the light signals above the door from the Pilot/Navigator telling them when to despatch the load. Firstly, the Red light would come on telling the RASC AD Crew to prepare for the drop, then the Green light telling them when to despatch the loads out of the door.

The Number 1, 2 and 3 despatchers always wore safety harnesses and were hooked onto the aircraft. In the photograph you can see that George is in the Number 2 position and that the safety harness around his waist is hooked up to the high safety wire. The Number 1 Position was i/c of the AD Crew and was usually an NCO. However, this position could be trusted to the more experienced Air Despatchers who hadn't been promoted at the time, particularly when the unit was short of NCO's. George had filled this position on many occasions when he was just a Driver. The Number 3 in the Team was positioned at the rear of the despatch board; Number 4's job was to drag the packs from inside the aircraft to the board, where Numbers 2 and 3 would then lift them onto the despatch board. When the green light came on, Numbers 1, 2 and 3 would lift the board, which sometimes held a couple of hundred pounds in weight, (approximately 14 Stone in comparable weight).

Usually, only two packs would be despatched on each run over what were often very small DZ's, and they were frequently surrounded by high trees and on those type of sorties, multiple DZ's had to be found. The soldiers on the ground regularly felled a few trees to allow for a larger DZ and they either released a tethered coloured balloon, or fired off a smoke grenade to identify exactly where they were located.

During his posting to 55 AD Coy RASC, George decided to try out for his Army Parachute badge qualification at Changi airfield. It would require him to do eight parachute jumps from both an RAF Twin Pioneer aircraft and a couple of jumps from a larger RAF Hastings Aircraft. There wasn't any military fitness training required by the thirty candidates attending the parachute course. They simply had to cover the background information and safety information on Parachuting and of course the essential Ground Training. The Ground Training was provided so that those doing the Course knew how to land properly using a parachute; without breaking either a leg, an arm or more crucially, their spines.

All of the ground training and jumps were supervised by RAF Parachute Jump Instructors (PJI's). The Parachute badge was humorously referred to as the 'Light Bulb' – (*by other soldiers who hadn't done any parachute jumps),* and was worn on the lower left sleeve of a soldier's jumper or uniform Jacket. When George eventually passed 'P' Coy and he became a fully-fledged Paratrooper with 63 Parachute Sqn RCT, he never wore the Light Bulb badge because it was always scorned by other fully qualified Paratroopers.

Changi Airfield was over three miles from Changi Point, which was where George was now accommodated as an Air Despatcher with Iskander Platoon at Telok Paku Point. He had to get up at

0500 hours every morning to walk the three miles from Changi Point to RAF Changi Airfield; it never occurred to George to apply for some accommodation at Changi Airfield so he wouldn't have to walk over six miles every day. Apparently, nobody told George he could have accommodation on the Course, and he didn't have the common sense to ask the admin staff. (*George's words, not the Authors*). George ate breakfast every day, because the 'walk' every morning really boosted his appetite. The 'Light Bulb' Para Course was run and co-ordinated by the RAF and each Course was run for both Army and RAF Air Crews in case they had to bail out of any stricken Service aircraft during their careers. George, tongue in cheek, says, "Turns out that most RAF Servicemen really didn't fancy jumping out of any Service aeroplanes, particularly one's flying at about 1000 feet."

The 'Light Bulb' Paratrooper Badge.

Although there wasn't a parachuting role for any of the units out in Singapore, a lot of Gurkhas and other Infantry units fancied having a go at parachuting and they signed up for the course, (probably just to check out their bottle for jumping from heights).

Another Serviceman from Seletar daily walked with George to the Course but stopped attending after he had completed his second parachute jump. The Course was for all Servicemen stationed in Singapore and it was joined by Gurkha's, Royal Marines, RAF Aircrew, and quite a few British Army Infantrymen who were also based in the Far East. When the other Serviceman dropped out of the Course, George had to walk on his own every day and part of the journey was past a Chinese Cemetery.

In the early hours of most mornings there was a ground mist near the cemetery and the small Chinese gravestones could be seen poking out of the still and eerie light fog. Combine that with the sounds of insects and bugs trying to let everyone know they were there, and George was often scared witless as he walked to the camp.

The lake that George walked past on his daily walk to RAF Changi. The headstones in a nearby Chinese cemetery really spooked him.

After completing his 3-4 days Ground Training, George took his first parachute jump from a small RAF twin engine aeroplane that could only carry twelve jumpers. They all jumped out of the side door in sticks of three before the plane had to turn back for another run because the DZ was very small. George had already volunteered to be the first jumper out of the door because he simply wanted to get on with the jump without anyone getting in his way just in case they hesitated. He also didn't want to be stuck behind a jumper who, as the Americans say, came up 'A day late and a dollar short.' He was also concerned about keeping clear of other jumpers after leaving the aircraft.

George says, "If I was number one out the door, I could get clear and after kicking out any twists from my parachute lines, I could concentrate on my landing without worrying about anyone drifting towards me."

Prior to his first ever parachute jump, George felt like he was walking on jelly as the RAF PJI called him forward and made sure he was properly hooked up to the static line system. The Jump Instructor shouted instructions in George's ear, "Red Light on….. Green light on…Go!" Without a seconds' hesitation, George immediately leapt out of the aircraft and shouted, "One thousand, two thousand, three thousand, four thousand - and check canopy." He kicked out a couple of twists in his parachute lines and started to look at where he was going to land. His landing was reasonable and after putting both feet on terra firma, he shouted, "WOW! That was just out of this world!" He couldn't wait for the aeroplane to land so he could complete his other seven jumps.

Brunei, Borneo and Indonesia

The Brunei Revolt in December 1962 was George's first experience of Active Service. This was closely followed by the Indonesian Confrontation which lasted until 1966. Both had their origins in the Indonesian opposition to the creation of Malaysia. At the start of the confrontation, Iskander Pln of 55

(AD) Coy RASC was initially based at RAF Changi and a varied and vast amount of military equipment was loaded onto RAF aircraft and flown across to the Brunei hotspot. Included in these items were Land Rovers and trailers that had to be driven up very steep ramps, then shunted at the top into the RAF Hastings aircraft. Lt Tony Case, the Pln Commander, sent two RASC soldiers off to Brunei to assist with the off-loading; one was a RASC Cpl and the other... George!

George was always issued with a .38 Smith and Wesson revolver whenever he flew over hostile areas in the Far East.

The main task in Brunei was a reversal of the work at Changi, e.g. off-loading stores from the aircraft, then passing it to the troops arriving to quell the rebellion against the Brunei Royal Family.

The purpose of the Federation of Malaya was to unite mainly Malaya and the populated states of the Malayan Peninsular, in particular the former colonies, Singapore, Brunei, Sarawak and North Borneo. In December 1962 President Sukarno of Indonesia tried to destabilise the process. He actively supported the North Kalimantan National Army (TKNU) in overthrowing the Sultan of Brunei and uniting the whole of Borneo under his Indonesian rule.

With direct support from the UK the Brunei Rebellion was quashed. Sukarno persisted hostilities by sending his troops across the border, with most of the action taking part along the border area. He did send paratroopers to drop into mainland Malaya, but again, they were quickly... neutralised.

The border between the then Malayan, Borneo and Indonesian countries was hundreds of miles long and in those days had fewer roads than today. Air supply was the most direct and efficient way of resupplying the border defence posts, so 55 (AD) Coy RASC started a rotational system of its troops between Butterworth, Seletar and Kuching. In addition to re-supplying troops with ammo, rations, clothing and water, the AD drops included live goats and chickens (to Ghurkha and Malay troops on the ground). Many of the drop locations were in very remote jungle locations far from towns/civilisation. In addition to the normal ration packs, individual soldiers could request personal items such as toothpaste, soap, razor blades, magazines, transistor radios, even beer (strictly controlled by ground units on Active Service – two cans a day per soldier).

All of these could be purchased from the NAAFI (Navy, Army and Air Force Institute) and would help to make life more bearable in the isolated jungle locations. These items were on repayment by arrangement of the soldier and the units 'President of the Regimental Institute' - (PRI). They were always referred to as 'NAAFI' items and were carefully packed into boxes and placed on the top of an air drop pack, which lessened the impact when it hit the ground.

Every pack content that was air dropped was carefully listed by commodity, e.g. ammo, fuel, rations/NAAFI, water, (even chickens and goats) then logged on a load sheet by the Air Despatchers.

It was not uncommon for a parachute to fail, (known as a roman candle), or for a pack to get hung up in one of the many tall trees, making the pack impossible to retrieve. Therefore, it was always useful to keep a record of what items had been lost in each pack.

It was always a mystery that when the No 1 Air Despatcher logged a pack that had 'Roman Candled' or was a 'Hang Up,' on a resupply drop, that particular pack was nearly always reported from the DZ as being the one that contained the NAAFI items. The No 1's sheet usually showed it to be a ration pack and not a NAAFI one.

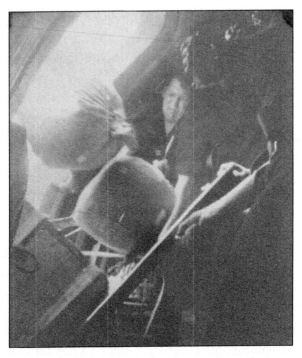

This Photograph shows George in the No 2 Air Despatcher position on the port door of a DH Valletta. The aircraft is approaching the DZ (Drop Zone) and two heavy boxes of cargo have been placed one on top of the other on the custom despatch board. The board has been raised to off-load the 'very heavy boxes' from the aircraft, as can be seen by the contortions on George's face.

Prior to the flight, in the Air Despatch hangar, each of the robust boxes had been packed with stores and had a harness fitted around them. The next stage required the Air Despatchers to transport them to the aircraft and load them into the main cabin and stack them in a certain sequence in which they were to be dropped. They also had to consider how many different DZ's there were to be supplied. All the stores were then lashed securely in accordance with the weight distribution limitations of the aircraft. Every aeroplane had its own unique loading plan.

When approaching the DZ, packs were unlashed, brought to the door and loaded onto the despatch board, in this particular picture two were being despatched together and then parachutes were attached.

Each pack had a weight limit depending on the type of parachute used, and in this case the 'R' type parachute is being used. The parachute is attached using 'D' rings on the pack harnesses and the two hooks on the base of the parachute. The hook and 'D' ring can be seen in the picture. A static line was attached and lead to the top of each parachute and then clipped onto a strong point on the aircraft floor.

When the aircraft was flying over the DZ and the Red, then the Green light came on, the board was lifted by the despatchers and the packs quickly ejected out of the door.

When the packs dropped away from the aircraft and reached the extent of the static line, the static line then pulled the parachute from its bag. When the parachute had been fully pulled from its bag the weight of the pack going down broke the tie on the parachute that was attached to the static line. The parachute then, in most cases, opened fully and landed on the DZ. The last thing for the AD crew was to pull the static line back into the aircraft before preparing the next load for the next drop run.

It was around that stage of George's military career that the RASC was deemed to be old-fashioned and in need of a change. The RASC was redesignated in 1965 into the Royal Corps of Transport (RCT) a slim-lined and modernised transport version of the RASC. George had joined the RASC to obtain a driving licence and yet he'd spent the first three years of his service flying in an RAF aircraft, over inaccessible terrain, despatching cargo out of them into the Malayan and Borneo Jungles.

This was exciting beyond words and very hard work, but between the heavy work they had some time for sport when in Borneo or Brunei. During light work periods, football or volleyball was popular. Volleyball was more popular as it could be set up easily and local leagues were organised in the base camps where they played against any other units in the area. The Gurkhas were experts and also provided an excellent after-game curry – they also had a plentiful supply of rum.

George remembers on one occasion loading his volleyball team into the back of the Land Rover and by the time they arrived back at their own base, the entire team was crashed out in the back of the vehicle and had to be carried into their basha's (accommodation huts). A combination of hard work, doing a tough job, and playing against a very animated and vigorous Gurkha Volleyball Team (and throw in a couple of Gurkha rum drinks) and it was all bound to take its toll.

Another team they played against was the Special Air Service (SAS). George had found out that their role was operating deep behind the enemy lines in the jungle to locate enemy forces and their bases. Also, they were feared by the Indonesians. He had also heard that the SAS were short of troops and were organising a selection course for potential candidates from the many British Regiments who were in Borneo.

CHAPTER THREE

AIRBORNE

George decided to find out more about this unique unit with a view to perhaps making a bid to join. He knew fitness was not a problem! He approached his unit 2i/c for advice on his chance of getting onto the SAS selection course. The officer was honest with George and told him that he didn't think he had much of a chance, as this was his first posting in the Army and that the SAS needed soldiers experienced in Infantry work. He advised George to apply for a posting to 63 (Para) Coy RASC. (_Author's Note_): _It was later that year that the RASC was disbanded to form the Royal Corps of Transport (RCT) based in Aldershot_. George would need some soldiering experience first, then, after a decent time, if he still wanted to apply to join the SAS he would be in a much better position to have a go at Selection.

The 'Confrontation' between Malaya and Indonesia officially ended when President Sukarno lost power in October 1965 and the nation of Malaysia emerged. This coincided with George's time in the Far East ending; so, with that sound advice received about getting soldiering experience, George applied for his next posting to join 63 (Para) Coy RASC. In November 1965 having completed his three years in 55 (AD) Coy/Sqn, George flew back to the UK.

On arrival in Aldershot, he reported to HQ 63 (Para) Coy RASC and was told to go on disembarkation leave until after next year, when it became 63 Para Sqn RCT.

P Company
63 (Parachute) Squadron RCT

In January 1966 George returned from his disembarkation leave and duly reported to 63 (Para) Sqn RCT.

It was mandatory in the Para Brigade (Bde) that everyone joining was required to do the very tough Parachute Regiment Selection Course. From past experience, 63 (Para) Sqn RCT realised that some of their Corps soldiers who were applying to join the Sqn had been employed in relatively sedate jobs and that they were not fit enough to pass the Para Regt Course; many good soldiers were failing as a result. To help these candidates, and in tandem with other support arms, (Royal Signals, Royal Engineers and RAMC Field Ambulance) had set up their own Pre-Para course fitness regimes, using their own unit Physical Training Instructors (PTIs) to get these soldiers fit enough to tackle the Para Regt course.

At that same time 63 (Para) Sqn RCT had a huge Physical Training Instructor (PTI), the very muscular and extremely confident Corporal Bob Ackerman, who was ably assisted by another tough PTI, Bobby

Cox. Famously, Ackerman and Cox taught and did PT differently.

One example was when their Pre-Para volunteers had to push a piano from Arnhem Barracks down Hospital Hill and into Aldershot town. They then went through Marks and Spencer on the High Street, and out the other side before being pushed/carried back to Arnhem Barracks. Although George didn't get involved with that particular event, he recalled that when doing pre-para training, whilst running on the course, they were banned from walking over any bridges on the Basingstoke Canal. Instead, they had to go under them hand over hand on the metal struts, then half way across each soldier had to hang by one hand and shout out his regimental number. He then had to change hands and do the same with the other hand. Anyone who was slow had to be overtaken by the guys behind him. Inevitably a bottleneck occurred and many ended up taking a bath in the Basingstoke Canal.

On one occasion, when a soldier couldn't hang on, he fell into the canal, but after shouting for help he was ignored by the PTIs; everyone then ran back to Barracks leaving him where he was. The next time George saw the soldier he was wearing a full leg plaster. He had broken it when he fell into the canal and onto a submerged metal frame that had been thrown into the water. He managed to crawl to a road and flagged down a car whose driver took him to the Cambridge Military Hospital (CMH). All credit to him, when George met up with him some months later he was wearing Parachute Wings!

Shortly after joining Pre-Para, George was deemed to be fit enough and was sent to do the Pre-Para Regt Course. Even to this day, he remembers the shock/horror he felt the first time he walked into Maida Gymnasium on Queens Avenue in Aldershot. It was the largest gym he had ever seen in his life and it automatically inspired fear of what was to come. Naturally, the first thing the PTI would shout was, "Right, twenty press ups for the last man to touch all four walls, Go!" After returning to three ranks the PTI shouted, "Not quick enough, do it again, Go!" The torture of P Coy was just beginning. Gymnasium sessions were followed by seemingly endless runs across the Training Areas including numerous trips up and down 'Heart Attack Hill.' George openly admits that he was never any good at running, but he just hung on in there and kept plodding. Eventually, the daily torture stopped for a brief time when the candidates were driven to Wales for 'Test Week.'

For George, the hardest part in Wales was the Stretcher Race, (designed to represent a soldier casualty) because in whatever direction you looked in Wales, it was uphill. Most of the time there, they were defying gravity. Mist, rain and sleet was constant. Nevertheless, he survived yet another phase. Back in Aldershot, the Log Race over the training area was extremely difficult because opposite him on the heavy log-carry was an older Officer from the Royal Army Education Corps (RAEC). It quickly became obvious to George that this officer was incapable of carrying a decent share of the weight but cleverly made it look to the Instructors as if he was doing his share. In essence, George was carrying both his own and much of the officers load, which meant that the log was lower than if two people were lifting it. George came to the special attention of a maniacal screaming Para PTI for not carrying the log higher.

He managed to get around the course but knew that he had done the work of two men, and the ignorant PTI SNCO was too cowardly to tackle the poor performance of the officer. The officer, though, did manage to get through the whole of P Coy. George realised, of course, that some flexibility had to be exercised by the P Coy staff or the Brigade would never have enough key personnel to operate properly. It was just bad luck that George was not switched on enough to avoid doing two men's work on the log. He is scathing, though, even now at the blinkered performance of the PTI. It showed him that being a PTI didn't need much brains, just the ability to run, scream and shout. *(Author's Note): The Para's needed to fill certain vacancies within the Airborne Bde, and it's believed that they did cut 'some 'slack' to those candidates who were 'marginally' less robust than other fighting Airborne Soldiers. Nevertheless, the Airborne Bde badly needed to fulfil replacements within their Units - even RAEC Teachers).*

The successful soldiers who passed P Coy were then taken to RAF Abingdon to complete the parachuting phase. Life was more relaxed at this huge RAF base, even though the tension and fear at having to jump out of a serviceable aeroplane made the course very stressful to some. It wasn't so for George as he'd already completed a parachuting course in Singapore (the one known derisively by other Airborne Troops as the Light Bulb Course). So, the parachuting jumps at Abingdon were not a problem for George as he could control his nerves better, because of his previous experiences. At the end of the course, George was presented with the 'full' set of Parachute wings.

Full British Paratrooper Wings Issued to Airborne Qualified Soldiers of all Regiments and Corps in the British Army.

The Parachute course in Singapore had entitled him to wear the Light Bulb Badge, the khaki balloon shaped badge with a parachute emblem, worn on a soldiers' right forearm. George, today, still treasures his, but has never worn it, as in the Far East all soldiers wore 'shirt sleeve order.' He never wore long sleeves out there out in Singapore because it was always so hot. In Aldershot, it was just as well that he didn't have it on his sleeve, as it didn't receive any respect from Paras. It attracted the comment, "Anyone can jump out of an aeroplane, but not everyone can pass the Para course."

On completion of the Parachute Course at RAF Abingdon, George returned to Aldershot and was presented with the coveted maroon beret and then joined B Tp of 63 (Para) Sqn RCT.

The Military at that time was a relatively poorly paid occupation, so a bonus in joining the Para Bde was that the Airborne Forces were paid an extra £2 12s 6d a week, called Para Pay. *(Author's Note): For the benefit of our younger readers, that would be about an extra £81.89 a week). To* continually receive the Para Pay, Airborne soldiers were required to complete at least six parachute jumps a year, one of which had to be a night time jump. As RAF aircraft were becoming scarcer because of various operational matters and defence budget restrictions, a less expensive method of soldiers doing parachute jumps and maintaining their records had to be found. The RAF found a way round it by using cages suspended below the RAF's huge inflatable balloons. The cage could hold four parachutists, plus an RAF Jump Instructor, who accompanied each balloon lift. He despatched the Paratroopers from the cage when at a height of 400 feet. At the end of the day's parachuting he would be the last man out.

The balloon was raised on the grassed area to the west side of the Queens Avenue, Aldershot, or on Hankley Common, a DZ a few miles from Aldershot. George found it to be a much easier method of doing the required parachute jumps. Surprisingly, many of his colleagues in 63 Para Sqn and indeed throughout the Para Bde, did not like parachuting at all, in particular from the balloon. To them it was an unpleasant toleration of being within an elite unit. The alternative to the convenient balloon jumps, was getting up at OMG hour, then a long uncomfortable truck journey to one of the RAF bases to board an aircraft.

The easiest to reach was RAF Odiham or very occasionally RAF Farnborough (1.5 miles). The furthest was RAF Colerne, just outside Bath in Wiltshire, where the Hastings were based. It was not uncommon that after a very early rise, a long journey to Colerne, and a long wait, to then be told that the drop was cancelled as the airframe was unserviceable or it was too windy. This was difficult to accept when you see a dozen or so aircraft sitting on the aircraft pans doing nothing. The soldiers then had to trundle back to Aldershot during rush hour in the back of a Bedford RL 3-ton Truck; sometimes entailing a 4-hour journey. (*Author's Note*): *This timing reflects the pre-motorway days*). When the new Argosy, (an aircraft that retired from service with the RAF in 1978), was cleared for parachuting, it was an easier journey to its base at RAF Odiham, a few miles from Aldershot.

Prior to the jump, the paratroopers were standing in two single lines. One-line jumping from both port and starboard doors. The number of parachutists exiting at the same time depended on the size of the DZ. Large DZs, such as Everley Common on Salisbury Plain could take a large number of parachutists from each door. Hankley Common, or Queens Avenue were restricted numbers as the DZs were much smaller in length. The RAF PJIs in the aircraft thoroughly checked each paratroopers equipment was fitted correctly and that the parachute static line, which pulled the parachute from the bag, was hooked properly to the wire line secured in the aircraft. Also, that their personal equipment packs or Bergens were attached to their harness by quick release hooks and the pack suspension rope was properly attached to both the harness and pack, then coiled and stowed in its pouch on the harness.

When the parachutist exited the aircraft and his parachute had opened properly, he firstly checked his canopy was open, then that he was clear of other parachutists. If close to another para, limited steering away could be done by pulling down on one of the parachute risers. When clear, he reached for the equipment release hooks and pulled them to drop the pack which would then be suspended on the rope below him. Packs could be ridiculously heavy, as some soldiers had to jump with vital equipment such as a mortar base plate, mortar tube or radios. This was in addition to his personal equipment.

There was a variety of vital heavy and bulky kit that was needed on the ground. George always preferred to be the number one to jump out of the aircraft. The lights were above the open door of the aircraft and when the red one went out and the green came on, he was sometimes out of the door before the PJI shouted "GO!" He felt safer having a bit of space between him and the others, especially if it was a double door exit.

One reason was that on one particular aircraft, (C130), the jumpers were told not to try to jump out as far as possible, as it might lead to getting caught in the slipstream and possible contact with the jumper from the opposite door under the aircraft tail. This was possibly a fallacy, but he stuck to his own method of leaving the aircraft.

The types of aircraft that George has jumped out of during his time with Airborne and Air Despatch units were: Twin Pioneers, HP67 Hastings, Avro 78 Andover, C119 Flying Boxcar, Argosy, Belvedere, Wessex, Iraquoise, C130 Hercules, C123 Providor, Nord Nord Atlas, and the famous C47 Dakota, (Danish Airforce). Additionally, as a sport/free fall parachutist, he has jumped from a number of different much smaller civilian types of aircraft.

CHAPTER FOUR

ADEN

'B Troop, 63 (Parachute) Squadron,
Royal Corps of Transport '

Shepherd (A), Harrison, MacDonald (A), Henderson (A), Still (A), Steel, Moth, Allen (A), Jones, Gibbins (A), Gardner, Melia (A), Moore (A), Steele (A), Buckmaster, Parkinson, Gray, Sterling, Williams (A), Grey (A), Elder, Finlayson (A), Flint, Appleby, SSgt Kurylak, Lt PE Miseroy (Tp Comd) (A), Sgt Jones (A), Powell (A), Hunt (A), Corcoran, McFadden.

Not On Photo: Harley, Hunter (A), Crouch (A)

(Those with an (A) next to their name on the photograph deployed out to Aden. LCpl George Henderson RCT is in the rear rank, 4th from the left – see arrow).

Eighteen months after joining B Tp, 63 (Para) Sqn RCT, the Tp was tasked to support the 1st Battalion the Parachute Regiment (1 Para) who were deploying to Aden. They were going to assist 1 Para in the enforced withdrawal of British Forces from the crumbling colony of Aden in the South Arabian Peninsula. (_Author's Note_:) _B Tp members were the only soldiers from 63 (Para) Sqn RCT that actually deployed out to Aden)._

Egypt's President Abdul Gamel Nasser was actively diminishing any European influence in the Middle East and was a major influence in Aden becoming an increasingly more violent and dangerous place for Europeans to live. Several peaceful attempts to hand over influence to an Adeni administration had failed miserably and a peaceful withdrawal was hampered by the many different internal Arab disagreements. Power struggles between the different Arab factions began, mainly the Front for the Liberation of South Yemen (FLOSY) and secondly, the National Front Liberation Party (NFL).

Prior to their departure from the UK, in preparation for their task, the Paras went to Sennybridge Training Area in Wales to practice their military skills and zero in their weapons on the ranges. Sadly, that coincided with the terrible tragedy in which over 140 people were killed (mostly children at the local school) when a colliery slag/spoil heap collapsed onto the local village (Aberfan). Even though 1 Para was only twenty miles away, they couldn't give any assistance at the disaster because they were deploying on an Operational Tour and had to complete the vital training needed for their Active Service deployment. Thankfully, other troops in the area were available to assist.

The Para Bn and their Airborne support elements were flown out to Aden in RAF Britannia Aircraft and on arrival, some B Tp members were 'blistered on' to each of their respective Para Company's. George was with Ron Macdonald in A Company.

The Battalion was based in Radfan Camp, just north of RAF Khormaksar and south of the notorious Sheikh Othman District.

The newly arrived Paras, including 63 (Para) Sqn RCT, were to be responsible for maintaining control of the main thoroughfares of the highly volatile Sheikh Othman and Al Mansura districts. To do that they conducted an aggressive patrol system, establishing Key OPs (Key Observations Points) within the districts. Additionally, the main route from up-country Aden was through these areas and so checkpoints were established to the North of Sheikh Othman and on the beach road. Firefights, grenade and rocket attacks were frequent along those routes, and so it was hoped by keeping the main extraction routes from the North (up-country) open and manned, the British could maintain security and keep the attacks subjugated.

One infamous day, on the 20th of June 1967, George and his troop mate and good friend (also ex 55 AD Coy despatcher), Ron Macdonald had returned from Sheikh Othman with A Company personnel to Radfan Camp. Just before turning into the Camp they both noticed soldiers on the range beside the camp, firing their weapons.

As per good soldiering practice, they both cleaned their weapons when they got back to the accommodation and then walked to the Armoury to hand their weapons in, they heard a lot of low flying bullets overhead. Initially they thought the sound was from range 'Overs', but they immediately discounted that because high rounds would never be coming from that particular direction.

They then became aware that someone was shouting about being fired on by the Adeni Army across the road from Radfan Camp, the ranges and Champion Lines.

George and Ron quickly ran back to get their ammo, but there were further shouts telling everyone to go to their tents and remain inside. The 'not to' fire command: 'weapons tight' was also being given. All of the tents had sandbags surrounding them up to waist height, so it was a relatively safe area in which to remain.

Sadly, some soldiers from 60 Sqn RCT were returning from a range day in Bedford RL trucks and were being shot at. The Adeni Police and Army in Crater had started an incorrect rumour that the British Army were shooting at them, which simply wasn't true. As a result of that information, 60 Sqn RCT's Range Party was fired at, resulting in eight of their soldiers being killed and another eight badly wounded.

Driver Billy Hunter of 63 (Para) Sqn RCT was awarded an MID (Mentioned in Despatches – with the Oak Leaf Cluster, for Gallantry) for driving an armoured Bedford RL truck which was tasked to go to Champion Lines and take over the armoury that was caught up in a fire fight. On the way across the open ground, the truck came under heavy fire and became immobilised as the tyres were shot out. Some of the rounds were coming in through the small front window hatches and ricocheting inside the vehicle. Billy was hit several times by shrapnel.

The hatches were lowered, but one, due to being hit by rounds, would not close properly. The quick-thinking officer in charge picked up a piece of cardboard and placed it over the hatch. The firers, thinking the hatch was closed, stopped shooting.

Shortly after a frontal assault from the vehicle to the Guardroom was then made by the paras; they achieved their task. The officer was awarded a Military Cross and Dvr Billy Hunter was awarded a Mentioned In Despatches. Billy was wounded in several parts of his body during this action.

During their time with A Coy, George and Ron were fired upon several times whilst out on patrol and on stag duties. George had also taken Para Regt soldiers out on patrol in Sheikh Othman and had been a member of fighting patrols in Al Mansoora. On one notable occasion he was No 2 on a General Purpose Machine Gun (GPMG) position on the roof of a building at the North Checkpoint. This position was established to keep the road from the North (up-country) open. Firefights were very frequent on that position and this particular night was no exception.

As another firefight began, George was directing the return fire from the GPMG at the enemy when he noticed a figure running forward from the base of their building, heading towards another building a short distance ahead. Despite the darkness, George immediately recognised the individual who was bravely going out to see if he could get one of the nearest enemy shooters. At the same time, George saw the barrel of the GPMG going down; he immediately used his hand to push the barrel away and at the same time shouted, "DON'T SHOOT, HE'S ONE OF ...brrrrrb... OURS!" Unfortunately, George was a split second too slow and a four-round burst from the GPMG went on its way towards the runner. George watched the individual flip over like a cart wheel. Thankfully, he was hit only once in the shoulder. The casualty later said that it was like being hit by a sledgehammer and acknowledged that he should never have gone out in front of his own guns without first letting them know what he was intending to do.

At that particular checkpoint, the soldiers were resting in a tent between stags when a mortar bomb landed and exploded in the sleeping area. George went into the tent after all the casualties had been evacuated and found one last soldier sitting on a camp bed holding an empty cup in his hand. He told George that after the explosion went off he was conscious of a hot sticky fluid all over his face and body. He thought that he'd been badly injured and was covered in his own blood, until realising that it was not blood but the 'NATO Standard' sweet tea he'd been drinking. *(Author's Note): For the uninitiated - NATO Standard Tea is a British Army milky white tea, heavily laced with at least two large sugars to sweeten the drink).*

Luckily, there weren't any fatalities from the mortar bomb explosion, but some of the other Paras did suffer from shrapnel wounds.

The political situation in Aden was continuing to change as the British departure neared. It had become a power struggle and armed conflict between the Front for the Liberation of South Yemen (FLOSY) and the National Liberation Front (NLF). At times territorial gunfire between FLOSY and NFL went on over the Paras Ops.

As the British withdrawal was now very near and the flow of military personnel and equipment from up-country had finished, key districts such as Sheikh Othman and Al Mansoora were evacuated by 1 Para and moved into the confines of Radfan Camp.

The security of Sheik Othman, vice 1 Para, became the responsibility of the Adeni Police.

A Battle Trophy in the form of an Adeni Police flag, taken from a Police station used by B Tp, 63 Para Sqn in Sheik Othman is now on display in the Aden Section of the Airborne Forces Museum at Duxford.

Radfan Camp was separated from Sheikh Othman by a series of Salt Pans and as a result was vulnerable to attack from the North. To provide a defensive line, 1 Para built a wall of sandbags across it with Observation Posts (OP's) at choke points. This was a mammoth task and involved filling many thousands of sand bags. It was nicknamed the Pennine Chain by Major (later Brigadier) Joe Starling, the 2IC of 1 Para.

George and Ron reckoned they'd filled almost all of them!

The handing over of British assets in Aden became well advanced. In Radfan Camp a massive clear-out of all of the accommodation stores that couldn't be taken back to the UK was being systematically sifted and if necessary, dumped. The local scrapyard was on the beach and as such British Army trucks were filled with all sorts of furniture which were then taken to the dumps and burnt. Some enterprising Arabs were in attendance at the dump and offered cash for each load on the back of the trucks before it was thrown onto the fire. It's possible that some Army drivers may have been tempted by the offers!

Radfan Camp was to be evacuated and the airlift of 1 Para to the UK via RAF Khormaksar and Bahrein began. All that was left was the many Army vehicles that were lined up along the camp roads. It was not cost effective to get these well-worn vehicles back to the UK. As agreed, they were to be driven a little way South and parked up in a huge compound ready for the Adeni forces to take them over. The Drivers (RCT and 63 Para) had to drive them in one large convoy to the compound.

As George started to move forward, the Land Rover behind him smashed into the rear of his vehicle, which shunted him forward and into the vehicle in front of him, which was Ron Macdonald's. Ron took exception and reversed his vehicle back into George's. This started a chain reaction and the rear ending and reversing was happening all the way down the line. The end product was most of the vehicles ended up being a challenge to the best Adeni Army Vehicle Mechanics (*the equivalent of our REME*) to get them repaired and serviceable. As a last defiant message, many of the soldiers didn't leave the ignition keys in the vehicles. No doubt they were jettisoned on the way to the repatriation RAF Aircraft for the flight home.

George, remembering his flight out to the Far East in 1962 and the blast of heat that came in when the Aircraft door was opened, now remembers Aden as being hot in many more ways than one!

Back in the UK, and after a good night's sleep in his old bunk in Arnhem Barracks, Aldershot, he arose to hear the voice of DJ Tony Blackburn on the former BBC 'Light Programme' now called 'BBC Radio 1.' He still listens to Tony on his 'Golden Hour' show.

George was also recommended for an award of 'Mentioned in Despatches' but because of an incident/disagreement with an Adeni Army Major his MID was changed to a 'Tie of Honour' Award.

CHAPTER FIVE

NORTHERN IRELAND

It was approaching Christmas 1969 and B Tp was on 'Spearhead'. This is a rotational duty that earmarked certain Troops to be on very short notice to be sent to any trouble spots, or emergencies anywhere around the world. A set list of clothing and equipment that every soldier needed to have was packed and ready for the off. B Tp, on becoming 'Spearhead,' had the usual kit checks. That is, checking that every soldier had everything on the kit list by seeing it laid out for checking by the Tp Comd. The emphasis of course was on all military kit being inspected and in good condition and serviceable when checked. Everyone was allowed to pack some civilian clothes in case there was some leisure time after the 'emergency callout' phase was over, wherever that may be.

George's friend, (and still to this day), 'PJ' was standing next to George, kit laid out when George noticed that he had got all the military kit as per list, but regarding the civilian clothes, he only had a T-shirt, jeans and flip flops. When George enquired, "PJ, Isn't that a bit dicey to have so few civies available if we get called out?" PJ replied, "Done so many of these and as you know; I've never ever been called out yet."

A week later, having been called out due to the 'Troubles' in Northern Ireland, our Tp was based in a TA centre in Lisburn. After a week of no action, they were allowed to go into the local pubs, which was in a safe area. PJ was shivering as he walked beside George wearing his jeans and t-shirt.

When George returned from the withdrawal of Aden, he remained a member of 63 (Para) Sqn RCT, where in his own time he decided to try another form of Parachuting. This was 'Free Fall', where the parachute was opened by the paratrooper by pulling a 'rip-cord handle' that held the parachute closed. This was different to how George normally parachuted, which was by having a static line attached to the parachute and the aircraft, which opened on exiting the aircraft.

One 'Free Fall' course George did was with the French Airborne, at the 'Ecole Des Troupes Aeroportees (French Parachute School) in Pau, near the Pyrenees in South West France.

These are George's French Paratrooper Wings.

The French Para Wings are metal, serial numbered and worn above the front right pocket of a soldier's shirt or combat jacket. If you are caught wearing a pair of these by a French Paratrooper, they will check the serial number on the reverse of the badge to confirm that the wings, and you, are not a faking Walter Mitty. You have been warned.

These courses were open to all units and on George's course he counted 12 different cap badges of British Army units. Notably, though, there were three members of the Special Air Service (SAS). One particular was the legendary (sadly late) 'young' Joe Lock, whom George had previously met at the Army Freefall Parachute Centre at Netheravon in Wiltshire. Also, there was Robbie and Pete; Pete asked George if he fancied attempting SAS Selection so he could be considered for service in the SAS. This was a bit of a surprise for George and unbeknown to him, the SAS were in Pau scouting for potential British military recruits to fill their ranks for **'OPERATION STORM.'**

On his return to Aldershot, with nothing to lose, George applied and went on the SAS Selection Course. It was not easy.

On the huge drill square in Montgomery Lines, Hereford, (bearing in mind that not a lot of drill was done at Montgomery Lines), George formed up with some 120 other men from various units, ready to start the Winter 'Selection' process.

The opening gambit began with something that is still fresh in George's memory, running around the huge square at a seemingly relaxed pace. After a few circuits, the leading SAS Instructor stepped to the side and was replaced by another Instructor. After about an hour of the tedious running, some members of the course were dropping out. They were immediately told to collect their kit from the billets and report to a clerk in the Admin Office. They were issued with a travel warrant and were told to contact their parent units for Return to Unit (RTU) instructions.

Some hours later, and like everyone else, George was beginning to feel the strain. He did not like running but knew that this was the game plan to get the unprepared/unmotivated, to drop out. Over the next few days the tasks got a lot more demanding. Map reading was an important part of the SAS Selection course, and it was clearly stated on the joining application to attend. Despite that, it was discovered that many soldiers, on arrival at Hereford, had limited map reading experience. The usual feedback was that the SAS Selection course was impossible to do due to their jobs in working units. So, lectures and practical tasks on compass and map reading were given. A few map reading tasks over the Welsh lowlands helped those weaker in navigation. It also assisted in building physical stamina much needed for the SAS test week ahead.

Some basic conundrums were added at certain points. For instance, George was handed a Chinese 'burp gun' (look it up) and asked if it had a safety catch! At another checkpoint he was asked another question. The answer he presented gave the Instructor a side splitting laugh; probably not side splitting now, but on a cold, windy, miserable wet Welsh day on SAS Selection at a check point beside a massive dam filled with water, it was. George was asked by the SAS Instructor how many lbs of explosives it would take to blow a hole in this dam? George replied, "I'd use six hundred and seventeen". The Instructor said, "That's very precise, how did you come to that conclusion?" He replied, "it's the number of the RAF's Dam Buster Squadron!"

Later, time and distance tests were introduced. By now the course had been greatly thinned down by dropouts who had seriously considered if they were ready and fit enough for the huge physical and mental challenge of the impending 'Test Week.'

The infamous 'fan dance' had arrived. The journey to the Story Arms Public House car park at the foot of Pen y Fan, in the back of a Bedford RL truck at 0400hrs from Hereford was cold but at least it wasn't raining. Bergens on, everyone started the slog. As George got higher up, the weather changed to light drizzle. As he got higher still it became colder and the drizzle changed to light rain. By the time he got to the first check point at the trig point on the top of Pen y Fan, he had gone through light rain, heavy rain, sleet, then hail, then snow, then a blizzard! His time checked and logged by the Directing Staff (DS) at the Trig Point, he continued over and down to the reservoir, the next checkpoint. The weather conditions remained horrendous.

As George was on his last ascent of Pen y Fan and as he was nearing the top, he saw through the heavy mist ahead of him, a dark shape that appeared to be on the ground. It could only be a soldier! As he got nearer, he shouted at him, "Oi, get on your feet!" Bizarrely, if George hadn't taken a slightly different route up the hill (nearer the Eastern steep edge) he wouldn't have found this soldier who was suffering from severe exposure. As he got level with the soldier and by checking his vital signs, with no response, George realised he was dead. In the appalling weather, after getting the soldiers Bergen off, he took the poncho out of his own Bergen and wrapped it around the soldier, all the time shouting for help as he knew the others on selection were passing him, but on the left of the mountain slope some 30 – 50 yards away.

George stayed with the soldier as long as he could, but when he realised that he was on the point of going to sleep and was not going to get any help, he knew he had to get to the top and down to the Story Arms to where the Army vehicles were parked.

On his way to the top of Pen y Fan George kept collapsing, this just felt like a blanket was thrown over his head, light to dark immediately... and after some time, he doesn't know for how long, he awoke and got back to his feet. After getting to the top, over and down towards the road, George was amazed at how he could sense the changing of temperature on his skin, it was also a complete reversal of the weather that he'd met on the way up.

On arrival at the road, he saw that the Army trucks had left, but a car was approaching in the direction of Brecon. George flagged him down and thankfully the driver stopped. George told the civilian driver to go to the Police and get them to contact the Military and tell them there's a soldier in trouble on the mountain. He informed the driver that he would wait and lead the Rescue Services to the soldier. The civilian driver said, "Get in the car, you're coming with me." Despite George's protests, the driver clearly knew what state of exhaustion George was in. What George failed to realise was the fact that he too was suffering from severe exposure and the driver had only just managed to decipher what George was incoherently telling him.

He helped George into the car and quickly took him to the local Police Station in Brecon, by which time George had recovered somewhat with the heat from the car's heating system. He gave the Desk Sergeant his map and pinpointed the exact place where the collapsed soldier was located. The policemen in the station then filled a bath in the Police-station with warm water and insisted George got in, saying he had done everything he could and that it was up to them to get things sorted from that point onwards. A Police Inspector even produced a bottle of brandy and gave George a taster, (not recommended for hypothermia but as George was in recovery, felt that it was helpful). Regardless, it certainly did help George!

The following day George was much recovered from his hypothermic symptoms. He then had to go to the local hospital to identify the deceased soldier. George was back on 'Selection' the following day and he continued on until he was finally 'Badged.'

When he'd passed SAS Selection, George went on parade with the other thirteen successful candidates where they were presented with their sand-coloured berets by the legendary CO of 22 SAS, Lt Col John Watts.

22 SAS had five Sqn's at their disposal. A, B, D and G Sqn's were based in Bradbury Lines in Hereford, and

C Sqn was based in Rhodesia, South, Africa until 1980, when that country became Zimbabwe.

All of George's Airborne Wings.
This set are the original ones belonging
to George Henderson.

The bulk of those on George's course were all sent to G Sqn and were told which Troop they were to join. As George was 'late' RCT he was automatically put down for 'Mobility Troop.' He made a representation that he joined the SAS for a change, not to do virtually the same job with vehicles. Thankfully, George had an ally in Sgt Steve Moores who was already in 24 (Air) Tp, and said that as he was already free fall trained, that he wanted George

Henderson in 24 Tp with him. (*Author's Note*): *George had met Steve previously at the Army Sport Parachute Centre in Netheravon doing 'fun' free fall parachuting).*

The following photograph of George was taken when he was still a Cpl at 63 Para Sqn RCT. He and other members from B Tp 63 Sqn RCT deployed to Belfast in support of 3rd Battalion Parachute Regiment (3 Para) whilst they were based in the Ardoyne. George was accommodated at the Ardoyne Bus Depot and he was aptly given a bed space in the depots tyre bay. During their tour in Belfast, George was contacted by a civilian called Colin Wallace who worked at the Headquarters in 39 Inf Bde (39 Infantry Brigade), Colin attached a couple of the 63 Sqn Paras to a free-fall parachuting team called 'The Bandits.'

'The Bandits' consisted of 14 Parachutist who were doing a KAPE (Keep the Army in the Public Eye) tour of Belfast and the two 63 Sqn Para's joined up with another well-known Army Catering Corps (ACC) Free-Fall parachutist to do some Charity events all over Belfast. The 'Bandits' team performed at Fetes and Charity Events all over Northern Ireland, hoping to raise some money for good causes.

Action Man in the 'Bandits' ACC, RCT & REME

PRESS RELEASE: ARMY PUBLIC RELATIONS, HEADQUARTERS, NORTHERN IRELAND

NEWS EDITOR
PICTURE EDITOR

Public Relations, Headquarters
Northern Ireland
Lisburn
Lisburn 5111 ext 521

3rd July 1973

THE "ARMY BANDITS" WHO
SAY: "KEEP THE MONEY"

To the Security Forces in troubled Northern Ireland they are "The Bandits". To others, "Knights in shining armour". They are an unofficial free fall parachute team of soldiers and a volunteer officer, who, since forming 10 weeks ago, have raised £15,800 for local charities and relations of troops killed in Ulster.

"The Bandits", a team of six who have all bought their own equipment and jump during their off-duty hours, have already put on 34 displays – sometimes three in one day – throughout Northern Ireland.

They have been seen by tens of thousands dropping from Army Air Corps "Beaver" aircraft and helicopters into playing fields, school grounds, hospital gardens, car parks and the sea near harbours.

Crowds at events have been boosted by their addition to the programme. But "The Bandits" don't take a penny.

At some fetes they drop from 7,000 feet with bouquets for Beauty Queens.

At children's events a two-foot-high (a doll that was popular in the 1970s but whose name is inappropriate to mention these days) falls with the team. Eager kiddies are allowed to keep the toy. "The Bandits" only ask for the return of its parachute.

Now the team are developing another novelty with child appeal – one of the parachutists drops dressed as a giant monkey.

All the members of the team are experienced parachutists who have made between 250 and 600 jumps each.

Says Team Commander, Colin Wallace: "Depending on weather conditions we normally fall 5,000 feet before opening our parachutes. A reserve one is carried in case of the 100,000 to 1 chance of the main canopy not opening".

But between jumps all "The Bandits" revert to their normal role in the Security Forces like 29-year-old Corporal George Henderson getting the "Your-my-hero" look' from a small Irish boy after dropping in at a fete.

He is a motor transport section commander helping to keep the vehicles of the 3rd Battalion The Parachute Regiment on the road. A member of 63 Parachute Squadron, Royal Corps of Transport, from Aldershot, he has made 300 parachute jumps since starting parachuting with the Army in 1963.

George's parents live in Pollokshaws, Glasgow, and his wife Susan in London.

She too is a free-fall enthusiast and has made nearly as many jumps as her husband with a civilian sky-diving team.

END

N.B. News Editor: Further details about the team can be obtained from the Team Commander, Colin Wallace, on Lisburn 5111 Extns 2216 or 2419

The full addresses of Cpl. Henderson's parents and wife are: 215, Shawbridge Street, Pollokshaws, and 29, Whitcomb Street, London W.C. 2. For security reasons it is requested the full addresses are not published.

These addresses are no longer relevant to George and Susie.

CHAPTER SIX

DHOFAR

All new arrivals into the SAS normally go straight out to the Far East to do jungle training, which is part of the normal SAS Selection process. This, however, was put on the back burner as the Regiment (Regt) was now committed to a more important job in the Middle East. George's entire selection course was needed to bolster the numbers in the Sabre Squadrons as the SAS had another urgent role to play in yet another urgent war... this time in Dhofar.

The secret war in Dhofar is far too complicated to go into detail in this book, but I will give you a brief resume so that everyone has an idea of what George and his SAS mates were up to in Dhofar.

Between the years of 1963 and 1976, the British Government covertly provided officers and soldiers from all three Services to the Sultan of Oman to help him quell a civil war that arose in Oman. The 'Dhofar Rebellion' was eventually quashed by a combination of Omani, Iranian, Saudi Arabian, Jordanian, Pakistani, UAE, Egyptian and British officers and soldiers. The majority of those forces were led by officers who were from all branches of the British Armed Forces, but in particular, Royal Marines and trained British Infantry officers who served in units like the Desert Regiment, Muscat Regiment, Jebel Regiment and Northern Frontier Regiment, amongst many other units and Corps.

The British Special Air Service (SAS) was also at the heart of suppressing this uprising and in particular Captain (Later Brigadier) Andrew Massey L/RCT MBE (Jan 1980) OBE (Jan 1988) Mentioned in Despatches (Apr 1994 for services on 'OPERATION GRANBY' Granby). Capt Massey did a total of three tours for the Sultan of Oman in Dhofar and ultimately ended up as the CO of 22 SAS Regt and was an instructor at Camberley where he led the Special Forces Counter Revolutionary Warfare Team (SF CRWT).

George Henderson knew Andrew Massey very well because he served with him in 63 (Para) Sqn RCT, in the Dhofar War, in the SAS, as well as at the RCT Depot and Training Centre in Aldershot. "He was a great guy and the man was an absolute gentleman" says George, who continues, "I once knocked his front teeth out whilst we played rugby at 63 (Para) RCT. He simply spat the teeth out onto the rugby pitch, picked them up, put them in his pocket, wiped his mouth on the sleeve of his rugby shirt and simply carried on playing; he was a truly tough guy." This was not a deliberate act of violence from George Henderson towards his own Brigadier, merely a badly timed tackle.

Captains Errol Harries RCT and Bob Birrell RCT were two other RCT Officers who actually commanded Infantry Company's during the shooting war in Dhofar.

Captain Bob Birrell's location during the Dhofar Rebellion was on the border with Yemen, which was a few hundred miles north of where the Aden Campaign was lost by the British. (*Author's Note*): *to be fair, the British Army was fighting against a Yemeni Terrorist Organisation supported by both Communist China and the Soviet Union*). The British led Company sized outposts were all that stood between the attacking Communist organisations in Yemen and the rich oil fields in Oman. If the oil fields fell into Soviet hands, then certainly other Organisation of the Petroleum Exporting Countries (OPEC) would surely fall the same way. It was an extension of President Eisenhower's Communist Domino Effect.

When Captain Errol Harries RCT completed his contract with the Sultan of Oman, he returned to the British Army and took command of 1 Sqn RCT based in Colchester, Essex. Within a couple of years, though, Capt Errol Harries left the British Army, yet again after signing another contract with the Sultan of Oman and then continued fighting in the Dhofar War for a number of years. After commanding 1 Sqn RCT, the British Army wanted him to attend Staff College so that he could progress further up the rank structure, but after fighting in a proper shooting war, the logical assumption is that everything must have paled by comparison for Major Errol Harries RCT. (*Author's Note*): *let's face it, nothing can possibly compare to the adrenalin rush of having enemy soldiers trying to kill you day after day*).

Captain Bob Birrell RCT (later Lt Col) describes Captain Errol Harries RCT (late Major) as being, "A lovely chap who unfortunately died some years ago on 30th August 2016. (*Author's Note*): *I interviewed Lt Col David Robertson (Bob) Birrell, late RCT and RLC a couple of years ago, and included a lot of Lt Col Birrell's entire military history (including some of his time in the Dhofar War) in a book called 'Soldiers On Wheels'*).

Until the British quietly gave a helping hand, the Sultans' Forces were poorly equipped with World War Two small-arms, and its soldiers didn't have many professional military leaders. The Sultan of Oman, who had himself been trained at the Royal Military Academy (RMA) Sandhurst, desperately needed help to defeat an organised Communist backed regime determined to take over his country. Bob's and the other outposts were less than five hundred miles away from Aden, which fell under the Communist/Terrorist pressure in 1964. The Sultan's hired officers and men were fighting against an enemy force that was simply referred to as the Adoo (an Arabic word meaning enemy or foe). The Adoo were trying to force the Sultan's Army back so they could have control of the **Hormuz Straight**.

Fourteen oil tankers (which is an estimated seventeen million barrels of crude oil), passed through the Straits of Hormuz every single day (which represented 35% of the world's oil shipments), through a gap which was less than 30 miles wide, making the Straits of Hormuz a very strategic location in relation to the world's seaborne oil shipments. George Henderson, Andrew Massey, Bob Birrell, Errol Harries and David C Arkless were just a few of the RCT soldiers who were there to simply stop that from happening. (*Author's Note*): *David C Arkless was an RCT Air Despatcher who had flown resupply sorties in Dhofar 1971-1972).*

The job spec of Air Tp in the SAS was aimed at getting Free Fall trained soldiers to infiltrate a foreign country by air. The Tp would use a method called High Altitude Low Opening (HALO). The team would jump from a military aircraft at high level, then when near the ground open their parachutes and float down onto a pre-determined Landing Zone (LZ) picked from an aerial photograph or map.

Once on the ground, as in old war films, the soldiers would stow/bury their parachutes, then get to their target to do the job.

Another method was High Altitude High Opening (HAHO). Using modern day parachutes and where a aircraft follows along a border, a team jumps and opens immediately at very high altitude. With modern parachutes that can cover great distances and turn across the border into enemy territory.

The Radar footprint of an SAS Trooper who is in HALO mode, is a very small one and he would only be spotted if the radar operator was looking directly at him on the screen, and only then if he was a very experienced radar technician. He'd also need to be looking in exactly the right place on his scope, at exactly the right time. Again, once on the ground, parachutes would be stowed then tasks done. The parachutes were merely a means of transportation into the country.

After George had successfully completed the 1971 Winter Selection for the SAS, he decided he wanted to be a Tp Medic and he qualified in that syllabus as his 'Basic Tp Task'. The Linguistics, Signals and Mobility skills would be tackled later, as George felt that being a Patrol Medic would be the most beneficial in the looming war in Dhofar. To qualify, he ultimately did a two-week stint of lectures and practical work in Hereford, then two weeks attachment in the Glasgow Accident and Emergency Department of the Southern and General Hospital. Thereafter he did others annually to keep his medical skills up to date.

George stated on his interview for this book, "There were no better places in those days to learn about the emergency treatment of injuries than in either a Glasgow or certain London A&E's. As, on Friday, (payday), and Saturday nights after the pubs closed, it was time to settle matters after alcohol fuelled disagreements! At A&Es he learned how to clean, then stitch wounds, give subcutaneous injections and safely straighten bones before putting them into a plaster cast." Attending operating theatres and watching surgeries performed also increased his knowledge. This also included dental matters. He related an incident during a leg amputation. During all operations, it is standard to count the number of swabs that are used. The used swabs were place on a counting rack beside the operating theatre table. After the amputation had been completed, the patients' limb was stitched and the amputated part was placed in a bag and sent for disposal.

The nurse counting the swabs used in the operation realised that she was one swab short. A search was done and the swab could not be found, a minor panic ensued! However, when the amputated limb was placed in the bag, George thought he saw something a bit odd on the amputated limb and said that it might be with the leg that was on its way to the incinerator. He ran to the door and along the corridors and was lucky to catch up with 'the leg' being carried by a porter. He looked inside and thankfully; the bloody swab was there. On getting back to the theatre, he was barred from going in because he was now 'contaminated.' Nevertheless, he was thanked for his recovery of the swab and observation. He has absolutely no doubt that the swab would have been found by the surgery team anyway.

During his placements at NHS Hospitals, George not only stitched casualties up, but he was also taught how babies were best delivered and what to do to keep them alive. It is evident that most women around the world are very resilient and that they are all quite capable of delivering their own babies. It's only when something goes wrong that they need and seek help. As an SAS Medic though, he needed to know what actually happened during the delivery phase of childbirth and the pitfalls that could arise. (*Author's Note*): *This Author was an RMA (Regtl Medical Assistant) during his time in the Army who had to deliver a baby in the back of an old white Army Bedford Ambulance. "I'd read all the notes and had been lectured about Emergency Childbirth, but nothing could have prepared me for the sheer terror of dealing with a new born baby's head emerging from a woman's nether regions").*

Whilst training in the A&E, George spent plenty of time learning how to cannulate patient's and how to administer Intravenous Infusions (IV's). He even attended Post Mortems. As bizarre as that might seem to most people, all really good Army Medics go through those procedures because it is an incredible informative learning curve.

George remembers one incident in an A&E where a poor woman had to come in every day for treatment, and he noticed that the other medics became very busy so that George had to deal with the lady. Her reason for coming in, she told George, was that she had to have an injection every day. He looked at her notes and saw that it was just routine antibiotics. He prepared the jab and asked the lady to expose whatever cheek she wanted the injection to be inserted. To his shock and horror, when she exposed her bum-cheek it was bruised black and blue all over and all down the upper leg. She said that the injections she was having were now excruciatingly painful, as of course was her whole posterior. George then realised why everyone else was suddenly very busy when she came into the Department. Nevertheless, he went ahead and chose the target and used the hypodermic as you would do throwing a dart at a dart board. It went all the way in and he pushed in the plunger. George said, "OK Madam, it's done." In a loud voice she said, "Oh my goodness, there was no pain this time, I hardly felt it." When she left, the others were looking at him as if he was a Martian! After this, George used his injection technique, (i.e. into the Arse Cheek!), many times with complete success. Along with 'X' marks the spot!

In 1971 George had finalised his medical continuation training in the summer, and within three months was sent to Dhofar on **'OPERATION STORM'** with G Sqn, 22 SAS Regt.

The Sqn split up into various locations around Dhofar and George's lot were to be accommodated in the famous British Army Training Team (BATT) House in Mirbat Fort. (*Author's Note): Readers should bear in mind that George's tour in the BATT House was only 12 months prior to the famous Battle of Mirbat in 1972.*).

'A' Sqn of 22 SAS was already in Dhofar and was finishing off their three-month stint. After his arrival in Dhofar, George and the three other SAS soldiers in their team climbed aboard a Skyvan airplane (nicknamed a bread van) at Salalah Airfield and were flown up to the dangerous small airstrip at Mirbat. This airstrip had to be cleared anytime a plane landed on it as the Adoo were planting mines. (*Author's Note): The Short SC.7 Skyvan was a British 19 Seat Twin Turboprop aircraft that was made by Shorts Brothers of Belfast. It was mainly used in Dhofar for short-hauling cargo and personnel as well as an Air Dispatch Aircraft to get food, water and ammunition to soldiers serving on the remote and inaccessible Jebels (mountain top).*

As George quickly got out of the Skyvan, a Scottish SAS soldier called Archie S, who was being replaced by George, was waiting for him to get off the plane. SAS soldiers knew it was unhealthy to hang about after disembarking from the aircraft. It was dangerous because they were more than likely to be mortared by the Adoo. Archie had served as a Paratrooper in 1 Para and he and George had served together during the withdrawal from Aden. They had a very brief conversation as they rushed past each other:

George: "What's it like here, Archie?"

Archie: "Shite!"

The BATT teams had taken over a detached house at the forward edge of the town. To the left of the BATT House (about 100 yards) was another detached building. This was the large 'Walis' (probably equivalent to a Mayor) House, to the left of that was the beach/sea. About 300 yards to the right of the BATT House was the Gendarmery Fort. Rows of barbed wire had been laid along the front of the Walis House, up past the Fort and continued around the town. The wire at the rear and North of the town had not been maintained, as townspeople needed access without having to go through the main gate between the BATT and Walis Houses.

There was a mortar pit a few yards to the right of the BATT House and beyond that, towards the Fort, there was an Artillery pit with a Howitzer.

Overlooking the town gate and Mortar pit on the front right corner of the BATT House roof was a sandbagged GPMG position.

Having made his way into the BATT House, George was getting his personal kit into one of the upstairs rooms, when there was a knock on the door. Outside there was a local man who spoke no English. All he kept saying over and over again was "Wain tabib, a'reed tabib.", which is Arabic for "Where is the Doctor (or Medic)."

Because George was the Medic, he went with the man taking his medical bag and weapon with him to deal with the emergency. On reaching the man's house he was shown a goat that had a four-inch laceration on its stomach. The gash had clearly been there some time and so suturing it wouldn't be possible because the skin simply would not bind and heal the old wound. The man started pleading to George, "Stitch, stitch, stitch!" George told him, "No, that won't work the wound is old." Instead, he applied some cleaning medicaments to the wound and administered a light breathable bandage in the hope that it might appease the local man.

The villager seemed to be suitably impressed by 'Dr' Henderson's diagnosis, treatment, and his overall bedside manner. George then returned to the BATT House hoping that this would not be the only requirement for his medical 'skills.' Sadly, George, the old man and his goat never met again, but George hopes it all ended well for them both.

The task of SAS soldiers (BATT) at Mirbat Fort was to recruit a fighting force of local men and train them to have basic military fighting skills, then arm them. At Mirbat, most of those in the Firqat were from the Bait Said tribe of Jebalis. The tribal areas on the Jebel were at that time under control of the Adoo and those loyal to the Sultan, and who wanted their area on the Jebel, back. *(Author's Note)*: *The Arabic word 'Firqat' simply means Unit. When the SAS talk about a Firqat they could be talking about a Company of 50 – 100 men or a patrol of just eight soldiers).*

One particular Firqat soldier that George had superintended as a Medic eventually went on to become a Doctor in Dhofar, after learning medicine in London. Said Salaim watched everything George did whilst they were out on the Jebel, and although not an academic young man, he spoke better English and Arabic than many other locals in Dhofar, he also spoke Jebali which he'd learned in North Africa before coming to Dhofar. George and Said, conversed for many hours and he found out about Said's family and his life before getting to Dhofar.

Said was a great help to George as he helped set up an Aid Post near their SAS unit's defensive perimeter whenever they deployed out into the field. Any Firqat's who required medical attention would report to the Aid Post and Said would help interpret their woes for George. If they needed any medication then George would give them an injection or any of the tablets that he had available. There was often a backlash though by giving one patient some medication, and not others.

The Arab diet was deficient in vitamins and the locals sometimes needed a B12 injection to boost their iron deficiency. Once one patient had been given a B12 injection, then others would congregate around the Aid Station, pointing at their arms and shouting, "Ibri, Ibri, Ibri!" "Injection, injection, injection!"

George states frankly that the Arabs are a very demanding populace and they wouldn't rest until they had been given exactly what the other bloke had received, whether they needed it or not. If the patient needed a shot of B12 then George would readily give it if he had some available, but if they didn't need it, he would give an injection of sterile water; a simple look into their eyes would give away the fact of whether or not they had an Iron

Deficiency. This worked on so many different imagined ailments, George stated on interview, "You wouldn't believe the super human effect a sterile water injection had on some of our Firqat's."

If George gave someone an aspirin tablet for pain, then he would have to give a different tablet for someone else because they didn't understand that the aspirin was for all pain, regardless of whether it was in the leg or the arm. In some cases, the Firqat weren't happy about receiving the same white aspirin tablet for a pain that they believed was different to the previous patients pain. Some SAS medics drew a small dot on the same sort of analgesic tablets using a felt pen and told the patient, "Look, it's a different colour to his, your pain is special."

'George administering a B12 injection to a local woman. The locals were renowned for having a vitamin deficiency because of their poor diet.'

The Firquat were a mixed bunch of soldiers who would sometimes stop during a firefight or patrol and start their Muslim Prayers. In the Dhofar War, it often transpired that brothers could often be fighting their own siblings because those that had come across to the SAS were fighting those that remained with the People's Democratic Republic of Yemen (PDRY). On another Operation, when George and Steve Moores were looking after the Coastal Strip, George states, "After working our way up the Jebel we started fighting the enemy and pushing them back from the East to the West whilst B Sqn, 22 SAS were to the North, (Right of us), and conducting a large offensive. The Adoo were on top of a dominant hill that we had to take. We advanced under accurate fire from the hill and were suddenly fired at from the North by a Machine Gun that George immediately identified as friendly fire from one of B Sqn's GPMG's.

A lot of the Firqat soldiers were Surrendered Enemy Personnel (SEP's) who had only come across from the People's Democratic Republic of Yemen (PDRY) to the Sultan's side, because they didn't like the brutal attitudes of the Communist soldiers who trained them. The Communist Instructors tried to viciously stamp out religious beliefs.

The majority of the Firqat soldiers were made up from Dhofaris who were historically suspicious and distrusting of outsiders and could, at times, be very difficult to work with. The SAS teams constantly had one eye looking over their shoulders because they had trained the Firqat how to use weapons that could easily be turned upon them. On the contrary, others had previously been members of other armies; some had held good rank. For instance, one member of the Bait Said Firqat had been a Staff Sergeant in the Trucial Omen Scouts.

There is an old adage in the Arab world that states, "If you find a Dhofari and a snake in your bed, throw the Dhofari out first."

George's first operation with the Firqat's, *(soldiers they had personally trained)*, involved a probing action to the base of the Jebel Massiff from Mirbat. They took a direct route to the Jebel Massiff where they started to climb for about a hundred meters. The Firquat were all moving fairly well, but George suddenly realised that a lot of their men had left their water-bottles behind and that they would have to return to the Fort to pick up the necessary water. The patrol had already been out for about five hours and it was beginning to get a lot hotter. As they returned across some sandy and shingle type ground, Steve and George hoped the return to Mirbat would be as calm and as orderly as the outward patrol had been. They travelled down a

Wadi (ravine) and onto some plain, flat ground that led to the base of another Jebel. At the base of that Jebel, the Firquat fanned out in their Sections and awaited the order to move as they had been briefed during their training.

At this time, the Monsoon period was still hanging over Dhofar. The furthest they could see through the constant mist on a good day from Mirbat was what was known as 'Jebel Alley', a rocky outcrop a few hundred yards in front of the Mirbat main barbed wire gate.

The BATT went there often, as there was a water well on its rocky top. Although there was a water hole in Mirbat town, the water from this tasted salty. The water from Jebel Alley tasted normal.

The well had to be cleared of mine explosives every day. Sadly, one day, the mine check was not done properly and one explosive went off under the foot of a local. JC, one of the BATT, got caught in the blast but fortunately for him, no lasting damage was done.

One morning when George was on 'stag' in the machine gun pit on the BATT House roof, he saw through the mist, a corner of the Jebel Massive (Mountain) known as the 'Eagles Nest' – it was a magnificent surreal sight. Each day as visibility improved the sheer scale of getting to the Jebel top became apparent.

The BATTs first operation with the Firqat was a tactical pre-dawn move to the base of the Jebel. On reaching it, they climbed up for about a hundred and fifty feet. As the monsoon period was disappearing, the daytime temperatures were getting higher, and by that time of the day they had been on patrol for four hours. Steve decided to get back to Mirbat, hopefully as orderly as the outward journey out had been.

At the base of the Jebel the Firqat fanned out in the sections and awaited the order to move back to Mirbat, as per their briefing. At that stage, George looked up and saw some people looking down on them, he asked, "Steve, we haven't left anyone up there have we?" Steve was emphatic, "No, they're all down here mate. I counted each one of them off the top." George and Steve suddenly looked at each other and said, "Shit!"

Suddenly, a hail of bullets came down on them. At that stage, George's training in the Malvern Hills kicked in and he ran the few yards back to the Jebel. He immediately dropped his backpack and took out the two-inch mortar and bombs he was carrying. He loaded one bomb into the mortar and aimed it at the Adoo. He pulled the trigger. There was a muffled bang and he watched the bomb rise about twenty feet in the air, wobble, then drop onto rocks and lay there. He fired a second round which was worse than the first. His intention of giving the Firqat some covering fire had failed. Looking around to see where the others were, he was surprised to learn that he was all alone! All the others had run from the base in the opposite direction and were giving covering fire in a Wadi 300 metres away. All he could do was pick up his heavy pack, loaded with useless mortar bombs, and start hot footing it towards the Firqat.

Dodging and weaving was out of the question because incoming rounds were hitting the ground on either side of George; he was committed to running straight towards the Wadi. When he got to about fifty meters from the Wadi, his right leg involuntarily shot forward and upwards, he then hit the ground. Weighed down by his pack, he thought he had been wounded.

He did a test, wiggle feet, OK, flex leg muscles, OK, thighs, OK. Everything else upwards seemed to be working. He realised that he was not hit, so with bullets pinging around him, he got up and again, hoping that one of them would not hit a bomb in his backpack he ran towards the Wadi. When he reached it and jumped over the lip he just lay there gasping for breath.

By that time Steve had radioed for Air Cover and two of the Sultans Strikemaster Jets had arrived on scene; they spotted some Adoo and dropped a couple of bombs on them, then did a couple of strafing runs which finalised the attack. One of the Firquat had been shot in the initial fire from the Adoo, so a Helicopter Casualty Evacuation (Heli Casevac) was sent for to fly him to Salalah Hospital.

Overall, this was an excellent contact. George realised some good points. The faulty 2-Inch Mortar and its Indian-Army sourced Mortar Bombs, were backloaded. Although George had fired quite a few practice rounds at Mirbat before the patrol, the box he opened to get this patrols bombs were useless. They were all ex-Indian Army issue! He immediately sent for an M79 Grenade Launcher to replace the 2" Mortar.

George and his Oppo coming down from the Jebel after another Patrol. Note: George is carrying his M79 Grenade Launcher that replaced the Indian Army Issued 2" Mortar.

Despite being told to carry and drink plenty of water during operations, the Firqat constantly ignored this Standard Operating Procedure (SOP) and put themselves, their SAS commanders, and probably all of their Operations at risk. They really did believe they were as good, if not better than, their SAS leaders.

Unfortunately, water was a constant problem for everybody, especially when they were on top of the Jebel, having constant advancing fire fights with the Adoo every day. Having four or five contacts a day on top of the Jebel disproved the myth about the Firqat not needing any water whilst out on patrol.

Following this patrol and arriving back in the BATT house, George inspected his boots and discovered what had brought him down was a bullet ricocheting from the ground that had struck the sole of his boot. There was a neat hole in the rubber sole, but he had avoided any serious injury because his footwear was American jungle boots and had a metal plate (anti-mine) in the soles.

This US design was manufactured to counter the very sharp Vietcong booby-trap spikes that would pierce their boots as they patrolled along the South Vietnam jungle trails. The spikes were smeared with human faeces so that the soldier would get a long-term infection and take him out of the war. (*Author's Note*): *George has had some problems with a displaced bone in his foot ever since the ambush and it remains problematic even to this day).*

(*Author's Note*): *When the British Army carry out Section Anti-Ambush Drills, they're always taught to charge towards the enemy whilst laying down as much Small-Arms fire as possible. These same rules applied to the SAS who practiced the very same exercises at Hereford. Even this Author did the same sort of training at the Jnr Ldrs Regt RCT in Taunton (1975). I have to tell you, dear reader, that life never goes the way you want it to, especially when 'It hits the fan.' It's a bit of a cliché these days but it's well worth repeating, 'No plan survives the first contact with the enemy.' The same applied to Tpr George Henderson on that day in Dhofar, although fortunately only one was injured during this encounter with the enemy).*

On the commencement of the major offensive on the Jebel Top, George recalls, "After tabbing along to the base of the Jebel in fighting order with Bergens, the BATT and Firqat climbed to the top. It was, to say the least, hairy at times. Steep, loose rock and very narrow animal trails. We linked up with the BATT and Firqat from Sudh, (a coastal town further North from Mirbat). We then started the long march to the West. We were the divisionary force to push the Adoo from the Eastern area to the central area where B Sqn, who were assembling at Jib-Jat Airfield to the North in the Central Belt, would begin advancing South to ambush the Adoo.

From the time we got to the Jebel top, resistance from the Adoo was fierce all the way. There were many contacts, (firefights), day and night. As we advanced, we were taking over and depriving the Adoo from vital water holes on the Jebel top. After two days of sitting over the water source the Adoo contacts started to reduce, sometime down to two a day." Strange as it seemed, George said that he could almost set his watch on the timing of these latter attacks, around 0900 hrs and 1600 hrs. He imagined it meant the travelling time from the Wadis' bottom to the top, firefight, lunch, firefight then back down to the Wadi before last light!

The reduced attacks indicated that the Adoo had no alternative but to move. The BATT tabbed ever Westwards.

When the BATT got to the Central Area, they neared a high hill that seriously overlooked their position. The Adoo were on top and started battle. Below it and dangerously exposed, it was clear the SAS had to take it. So, advancing under accurate fire from the hill, things got much worse as suddenly, they were being fired on from their right, the north. The main fire was from machine guns. George says, he knew immediately that it was from B Sqn GPMGs as they were known to be to their North. The rounds were just inches too high, thank goodness, as the sheer power of these bullets flying past was terrifying and there was absolutely no doubt whatsoever of their potential deadliness. Regardless, the immediate task meant there was nothing they could do but continue the attack on the hill. The firing from the North stopped after George threw a blue smoke identification grenade. It then began ranging on the hill above and ahead of them. On reaching the base of the hill it was a steep climb to get to the top as quickly as possible. George fired many rounds of M79 Grenades onto the ridge line above and was pleasantly surprised and relieved to see B Sqn 81mm mortar bombs also landing on the top. The nearer they got to the top there was less Adoo fire. As per a classic attack, B Sqn timed it perfectly to cease fire as they reached the apex and took over this dominating feature.

Six weeks into their tour, George and Steve were out on another Jebel, heading East and fighting the People's Democratic Republic of Yemen (PDRY). There were about 16 SAS soldiers out on that fighting patrol ,(about eight per Firqat), when they started taking some incoming fire. George threw a smoke grenade to identify who they were because he recognised the sound of the rounds and realised, they were coming from a British 7.62mm GPMG (General Purpose Machine Gun). It was friendly fire that they were taking. The incoming friendly fire soon abated and its aim was raised up to the top of the hill that they were assaulting, (the Northern Group) and after taking the hill it started to get dark.

The assaulting group (AG) went slightly back down the hill, spread out and settled down for the night, with George and Steve covering the AG's right flank.

Shortly after, as night fell, they spread out defensively around the feature, but on its Southern slope and therefore out of sight and covering fire from B Sqn! Darkness began to fall, so Steve and George stopped on a small hollow about 150 feet below the brow of the hill. Everyone knew the Adoo would not let this hill go with ease. So, as expected, when dawn broke, the Adoo began their attack from a higher feature about 250 yards in front. With bullets all around them, Steve and George returned fire. Steve was using his rifle and George the M79. The incoming fire did not reduce, and they realised that it was only the two of them in contact with the Adoo. The others were some distance to the right and out of sight due to the terrain.

Suddenly, Steve fell onto George and said, "I've been hit." It was only a matter of time before George would be shot too as the fire was extremely heavy and accurate. George took a quick look at Steve's wound and decided that as there was no great blood loss, and no way that the Heli vac could be done in that dangerous position, the only thing to do was to get him to the top of the hill as quickly as possible. Steve would need evacuation to the Field Surgical Team (FST) in Salalah.

No lightweight, George had to drag Steve up the steep slope by standing over him and lifting him by the armpits then moving him a foot at a time. Once again, the Henderson magical shield appeared, although the firing was heavy, they were not hit. About a third of the way up, George's strength was fading and he decided to turn around, face uphill and drag Steve up that way. He thought that it would be better doing it this way, as getting shot from the front would be preferable to being shot up the arse!

Half way up the hill, he remembers the sweet sound of GPMG fire. Friendly gunners had moved to locate the enemy positions. Almost instantly, the firing on Steve and George reduced greatly and they continued to the top, onto a bit of dead ground and safety from any further Adoo fire.

A bullet had passed through Steve's radial and ulna bones in his forearm, and had entered his body between his sternum and navel, (near the Xiphoid Process), before lodging under the skin in the middle of his back. It wasn't a bloodshed gore-fest like in the movies because Steve wasn't losing very much blood at all. After dragging Steve to virtually the top of the hill, George heard the GPMGs giving covering fire, which took the heat off the pair of them. Whilst putting First Field Dressings over the entrance and exit wounds in Steve's arm and the entry wound on his stomach, George shouted out, "We need a Heli Evac (Helicopter Evacuation) now!" But he was told by the recently attached Infantry officer that it was too dangerous to bring the Huey evac helicopter in just then.

It was now safe to give Steve the best first aid possible. George got his water bottle out and whetted Steve's lips, but didn't allow him to drink any significant amounts of water. Steve was a casualty in serious shock and he couldn't be allowed to drink anything because that would cause him further complications. By whetting his lips, George was relieving Steve of some of the shock symptoms. When Steve said that he was in pain, George administered a syrette of morphine to his friend, Sgt Steve Moores SAS, who remained coherent and lucid throughout this whole experience - and all the while he was still giving orders to his Firqat. George stated quite categorically that Steve was incredibly brave during the firefight and that he was still motivated, despite being seriously wounded.

Although George knew he couldn't give Steve anything to drink before he was evacuated off the hill, he continued to try and find a decent vein to put an IV (Intravenous) line into him. George was considering doing a cut down procedure because Steve was close to going into Peripheral shut-down. Had that happened, George would have to cut through the skin in his ankle and probe down with a pair of Spencer Wells Forceps to find a vein that could be used for canulating an Intravenous Infusion Line. Luckily, George found a decent vein, with enough pressure in it, and he managed to get a cannula into Steve. He was then able to put some desperately needed fluids into Steve's circulatory system.

Realising that Steve was seriously wounded, George shouted to the Tp Comd that a Helicopter evacuation was urgently needed. He was told that unfortunately it was simply too dangerous to bring the Huey evac Helicopter in at that time. After a short time, George demanded the much-needed helicopter NOW! Within minutes the helicopter, that had been alerted and was standing off, arrived and landed on the ledge near to where George was positioned and took Steve on the short flight down to Salalah Airfield, where an Field Surgical Team (FST) was based. The FST went to work on Steve immediately after the Huey landed and word got back to George, and the other SAS soldiers still up on the Jebel, that he was definitely going to survive and would soon be flown to British Military Hospital (BMH) Cyprus for further treatment.

Tragically, Steve died during the transfer from Salalah to BMH Cyprus, a place where he would have received definitive care. The reasons for this are numerous and very complicated to put into print and an awful amount of guesswork is involved. (*Author's Note*): I *consulted with a Senior British Paramedic who not only performs, but also arranges and co-ordinates critical care and aeromedical transfers. He took an hour out of his busy schedule to give me his personal opinion of what could possibly have happened to Steve:*

A 'Modern Day Assessment of 'Sgt Steve Moores wounds and his First Aid Treatment'.

Steve was treated by a field surgical team in Salalah whose role it was to triage and 'optimise' the patient for transfer to definitive care. An FST has only very basic facilities and resources, having been designed to be highly mobile and to provide excellent basic care for large numbers of casualties before transferring them to a larger and better equipped facility.

Due to the trajectory of the bullet, it was probable that significant injuries occurred internally that required complex surgical procedures to repair, sadly something that is not available in the field. In this case, what would eventually become known as an A, B, C, D, E approach would be adopted, along with rapid transfer to definitive care.

Critical care aeromedicine was in its infancy at the time of the Dhofar War and as such, whilst the Treating Team would have been experts in their field, they didn't have access to the kit and other equipment that would come along in time, allowing the delivery of hospital level care and treatment in transit like the Medical Emergency Response Teams

(MERT) that operated daily in Afghanistan in more modern times.

Steve was potentially hypovolemic (in shock), meaning that his oxygen carrying capability had been impaired. Now, factor that into him being placed inside an unpressurised aircraft and then taken to an oxygen deficient environment where he could well have become hypoxic.

Oxygen is essential to all life. As recent effects have demonstrated, if you can't get oxygen onboard and can't transport it to the organs, patients will die. Hypoxia (low oxygen) coupled with hypovolaemia in an already severely compromised patient is something that requires immediate and specialist treatment in a facility designed to manage the major trauma. If you were to roll forward in time to combat events in the not-too-distant future (Vietnam) these facilities were moved closer to the front line and combat casualty survivability increased significantly.

That is all a hypothesis of course, because as explained, it is impossible to know the chronology of particular events, without having access to the medical notes, or knowledge of the treatments provided pre-transfer to work from. It is simply a personal theory based on a Paramedics modern-day experiences of similar situations, gained whilst evacuating patients from modern day conflict zones.

The Ministry of Defence (MOD) has invested billions of pounds into the delivery and care of critically injured soldiers from the battlefield since the War In Dhofar, and so it is difficult to speculate what would have happened to Steve in a more recent battlefield situation.

'Sgt Steve Moores SAS'

From the hill where Steve was wounded, the BATT made its way north into B Sqns location, as they had completed the tactical plan. They were now in the central area and new plans were being formulated for the next phase.

Shortly after arrival, a B Sqn soldier came over and apologised for shooting at them. He then asked where his shots were falling. George gritted his teeth and simply said, "About two inches too high!"

After two days, it was decided that the patrol, together with a much-reduced Firqat number and along with a company of Geish (Sultans Army), would move further west along the Gutn (Jebel top) and clear some of the Adoo known areas on Wadi tops. The reduction of Firqat was due to many saying their contract was to free their tribal area, which was now done!

During one Wadi sweep they were about to start going down the narrow ridge at the top. The ridge widens as you walk down and the Wadis either side get steeper and deeper. They started moving down. The BATT, numbering 11 by now, were on the right-hand side, George was number three in line, armed with a GPMG. The Firqat on his left suddenly stopped and had a 'tatib' (conference) then came over and said they wanted to change position and advance down the right side. As George says, "We always knew that if the Firqat wanted something - there was usually an ulterior motive, but we complied with them."

They set off again, it was becoming difficult to keep sight of the Firqat, now on his right. Eventually he lost sight as the ridge widened and the scrub and bushes were higher. Suddenly, a fire fight on his right began, he turned and ran over the hill and down to where the Firqat were doing battle. After a short time, due to the increased firepower against them, the Adoo withdrew down the Wadi.

Sadly, the Firqat had a fatality, one shot dead on the opening shots of the ambush ... he was the number three in line, who had taken Georges' place on the changeover!

The war was now changing as the Sultan had entered into defence agreement with Iran. These Countries were separated by the Gulf of Hormuz. The closest point between the two was just 21 miles.

The Midway Road from the North of Oman to Salalah had to be opened. Using the BATT and some Firqat as guides they managed to lead the Iranians to defensive locations from the plain up to the place called Midway. It took much longer than planned as the Iranians moved very slowly. It was unsettling watching the dawn coming up and still moving in line up the stony road. The Adoo were always quick to identify weak spots and so they were open to ambush.

George remembers in the Iranian position there was much shooting all around them, which was not coming from the Adoo, but from the Rock Sangers, the Iranians were using. It was part of their system to clear weapons when changing stag. The problem was some were shooting inwards across the defences and just missing the BATT.

When the Adoo started their attacks on the position, the firing around the BATT was coming from both directions, so a wall was built behind them, which was in addition to the wall facing the Adoo.

When things calmed down the following day, the BATT, as a gesture of what tactics they do, decided to do a patrol. George says, "We left the Iranian defensive position, and explained where we were going to patrol." The Iranians agreed and watched them go. "We were never out of sight of them."

After getting three hundred yards towards the first feature the Adoo opened up from a hill in front. George and their unit went to ground and returned fire. In the meantime, the Iranians who again had watched them leave their position and started patrolling directly in front and in clear view of them, started firing at George and his lads! Once again, a smoke canister came to their aid and the Iranians stopped firing, as did the Adoo, who had probably fired off all of their ammo. On the way into the Iranian position, the officers looked extremely sheepish. It also ended the example to them of war in Dhofar!

After another sleepless night of random firing, in the morning, George and his lads left by helicopter to fly to Um Al Gwariff, the SAS base camp in Salalah.

The Midway Road was now being opened and the Adoo, prevented from having free reign on the Jebel top, were moving further East but making good use of the Wadis to attack the Sultan's forces.

George became one of a fighting group whose task was to move further East. The groups march was led by a company of Jaish, the Sultan's Army and followed by as many of the Firqat who wanted to come. Many of them had left, saying they had finished the contract with the Sultan as their tribal area was now liberated.

The move was tricky as the Government troops were moving in line sending pickets to higher ground on the route. The BATT were at the rear. The Adoo, always capitalising on any mistakes made by the Sultan's forces were following on behind and sniping at them and, as though it was a sign of defiance, in full view!

Along the march route George remembers walking through the vacated Government forces positions and passing fires that were burning the excess equipment that could not be carried to the next position. This also included ammunition. A huge amount of live bullets had been thrown on the fires and by the time George and his group reached it, the bullet casings were exploding and the bullets were flying around, dangerously close.

At one stage during the war, George was firing a British 81 mm Mortar and firing 'mixed fruit and pudding'. This is a mix of high explosive (HE) and phosphorous shells against the enemy, unfortunately one of the PH shells was leaking and when he picked it up, he got a lot of the phosphorous chemicals on his fingers which burnt and blistered his entire hand. George put plenty of water on the injury before dressing the wound himself and then simply carried on with the rest of the mission.

George on the Jebel top with his Armalite personal weapon

George on a Jebel with captured weapons

Some six weeks later G Sqn returned to Hereford and, after 10 days leave, normal business resumed and the training courses for the other jobs that the SAS do, one of which was to complete the basic SAS requirement.

George only had about four weeks of his tour left in Dhofar after his friend Sgt Steve Moores had died on the medivac flight back to Cyprus. He and the rest of G Sqn continued with the campaign to push the Adoo back towards the Border, George and his Firqat's were by now located in a horseshoe shaped feature up in the hills with the ground sloping upwards from the South.

Three weeks earlier, George had lost the majority of his equipment when his Bergen had fallen out of the logistics helicopter that was moving their kit up towards their forward position. The Bergen had fallen down a Wadi and amongst other things, he lost his camera.

Because the SAS and Firqat were constantly in firefights with the Adoo, they needed a re-supply of water, ammo, and rations before they could carry on heading East. They had continued to dominate the water holes on the high ground to deny these 'luxuries' to the enemy. The wind was blowing from North to South and it was therefore a relatively simple Air Despatching mission. The aircraft would overfly George's position and deliver five different air despatch loads in an up-wind position. The parachuted cargo would then drift down wind and with a bit of luck, and judgment, they would land on their horseshoe shaped Landing Zone (LZ).

Things had moved on since George had been an Air Despatcher out in Borneo, the soldiers on the LZ were now in direct radio contact with the pilots who were dropping the cargo from their aircraft. George contacted the pilot in the Skyvan and after explaining that he was a trained Air Despatcher, he requested that the pilot work on George's commands.

The pilot agreed to work on George's directions and as the plane neared the LZ, George judged the winds to be very strong and gave the appropriate directions to the pilot. "Ten right…. Ten right…. Five Left … Red On…. Drop, Drop, Drop." Two packs on parachutes came out the rear of the aircraft and started to drift down towards the LZ.

The Firqat's mortar tubes were sighted in the bottom of the horseshoe location and the shells landed right next to the mortar bay. George modestly states that the drop was, "Quite easy really," and that he couldn't get it wrong even if he'd tried. The next load was the rations that consisted of rice and tinned meat for the Firqat's and it landed half way up the hill which was precisely where it was needed. The last load consisted of the water and that landed just inside the lip at the top of the horseshoe, which was where a lot of the soldiers were positioned on sentry duty.

George states, "It was one of the most unique air drops I'd ever witnessed, absolutely everything landed exactly where it was needed. Although I was giving directions to the pilot, I had no idea of what was in each airdrop and all six re-supply cargos were ultimately delivered with precision, to exactly the right location. After receiving all of our stores, we had to do very little humping and dumping." As an ex RASC Air Despatcher, George is very proud of this achievement.

George and the other SAS soldiers were ultimately helicoptered out of the field and taken to the SAS Base Camp at Um Al Gwaiff where they enjoyed hot showers and shaves before flying off to Mazeira (Masirah) Island just off the coast of Oman before flying to Cyprus and then back home to the UK. Suzie was living in a flat in Brighton at the time because she was a commercial KLM Airline Pilot who flew out of Gatwick Airport. Depending on who was doing what in both of their busy lifestyles, they travelled and met up in Brighton, Amsterdam or Hereford where they also had a Service married quarter. George was given access to complimentary KLM air tickets because Suzie was one of their pilots, and they often spent the weekend together in the Dutch capital.

Captain Suzie Henderson KLM

(Author's Note): A few years later George noticed that the Permanent Staff at the SAS Centre in Hereford consisted of more than a few soldiers with only one arm and some that carried severe limps. They all wore British Army uniforms and were employed in various jobs as Regular Army Training Staff at Hereford. George was informed that the SAS felt these injured ex-soldiers still had something to offer the Army and so retained them, regardless of how the RAMC Medical Boards viewed their physical abilities and status. The SAS always look after their own.)

CHAPTER SEVEN

BACK TO HEREFORD

Suzie and George enjoyed a couple of weeks leave after George had returned from Dhofar, he then returned to Hereford and got his kit ready for the Jungle Warfare Course which was held out in Singapore. To a degree, George enjoyed life in the jungle and he embraced its all-consuming, and stifling heat and vegetation. He'd already operated in the jungles of Borneo whilst serving with 55 (Air Despatch) Company RASC on his first ever posting within the Corps, but this time, George would be doing the SAS Jungle Course in Malacca, and under SAS guidance and scrutiny. The SAS jungle selection would be a lot more augmented and difficult though, compared to the relatively simple stuff he'd done with the RCT Air Despatch Sqn in Borneo.

Many avid military readers might believe that jungle training is similar to the sort of soldiering that was done in Burma during World War Two. Soldiers hacking their way through the thick jungle undergrowth with a machete in one hand, whilst sweating away underneath an Aussie type slouch hat in the extreme and harsh environment of a rain forest. For SAS soldiers like George Henderson and other members on his SAS jungle warfare course, things were now conducted somewhat differently.

They didn't feel the jungle was their enemy and they weren't merely surviving and noisily bashing their way through local bamboo-brush looking for Japanese soldiers. They now calmly embraced the rainforest and used its various elements for their own gain. Like the Royal Marines and other Infantry soldiers that trained in the Belizean jungle, George calmly accepted life in the jungle for what it was, and he felt at home in the all-consuming and stifling jungle heat. He even embraced the damp vegetation like an old friend. (*Author's Note*): *George and his other SAS mates; along with Royal Marine Commandos, are really just weirdos because they enjoy it in the jungle).*

Although George had yet to, technically, complete his SAS Selection Course because he hadn't done the jungle phase - even though he'd been out to Dhofar and had fought with the SAS in the Dhofar war. (*Author's Note*): *I remember serving with 2 RTR 2 (Royal Tank Regiment) in Wolfenbuttel, West Germany in the early 1980's and one of their Cpl's (let's refer to him as Cpl Jones…. mainly because that was his name) did selection before going on the jungle phase. Jonah had passed everything and had qualified as an SAS Tpr up to that point, but when he briefly visited his parent unit after 'Selection' he told his friends that if he hadn't passed the jungle phase at the first attempt, he would have sacked the whole SAS process because the jungle phase was a very physically draining and trying part of the final qualification. Incidentally, Jonah was tempted into doing 'Selection' by the now famous and deceased, Captain Danny West SAS, who was in Wolfenbuttel on a military sabbatical, his parent unit was also 2 RTR).*

There were thirty SAS soldiers on George's Jungle Course which included sixteen soldiers who were students looking to complete their SAS training,. The rest were SAS instructors and permanent staff who ran the Jungle Warfare Courses in Malacca. The background work in setting up each phase of jungle training was phenomenal, each Course had various modules and timetables that needed to be strictly observed, followed by certain goals to be achieved. The candidates were split up into different four-man patrols for the Course and each Patrol was accompanied by their own personal SAS instructor whilst out in the jungle. Initially, each Patrol was taught and trained in Jungle Warfare, Building Basha's, Navigation and Tracking and how to deal with the local wildlife.

One form of wildlife that never perturbed George while he was in the jungle, but has given many other men nightmares from hell, was leeches. During one stay in the jungle, George's mates counted thirty leeches taken off his body. The leeches were HIRUDO MEDICINALIS, the common black leech that can suck itself up to fifteen times its pre-feeding size on a human being. The largest one in the Malaysian

Jungle is the Bull Leech that can consume about one pint of human blood at any pigging-out session. All leeches are relatively harmless and most cannot pass on any sort of disease.

On the first day in the jungle, the patrols were taught about the difference between 'Hard' and 'Soft' routines. The SAS instructors chose a Grid Reference (GR) in an area that the Patrol had to find. The site always had a good water source and it also had plenty of hills to climb. The Instructors had been out to these GR's previously and had set up different camps, with areas for beds and general administrative duties. There was always a plentiful supply of trees, creepers (vines) and Atap (broad leaves) to help the students build an adequate and comfortable temporary shelter that they could use to provide themselves with protection from the jungle elements.

The next phase required the SAS candidates to construct the best shelter they could from using only the available local vegetation, some para cord, and an Army issue cloth hammock. Whilst doing that phase the candidates were constantly being given lectures on jungle tactics.

At one particular location, George went down to the stream to fill up the patrol members water bottles and he noticed a footprint in the soft, muddy river bank. It was a fresh tiger foot print, about the size of a huge serving dinner-plate. The SAS carried live ammunition on the Jungle Course just in case they needed to defend their patrol from wildlife. Their SAS Instructor was laid in his basha when George got back. He started briefing the course after George returned with the water bottles.

SAS Instructor: "Right, listen in! You are to patrol on the other side of the river from now and move tactically up the hill until you get to the Emergency Rendezvous (ERV) at Grid Reference 6741 3917. Remain hidden in that area for about 30 minutes after setting up a temporary observation post and wait until I get there before doing anything else. Any Questions?"

Patrol Candidates: "No." "No." "No." "No."

As the patrol hadn't got any questions, they started to set off towards the stream. They were still within earshot of their SAS instructor when George started telling them about what he'd just seen down by the water's edge.

George: "Bloody hell lads, you should have seen the size of the Tigers footprint on the river bank just now. It was a fresh footprint and of a colossal size. I've never seen such a gigantic Tigers footprint."

The Instructor suddenly called them back.

SAS Instructor: "What was that you were talking about?"

George: "There's a humongous Tigers footprint at the edge of the stream in our location. I was just about to say to the lads that I wouldn't like to bump into a cat of that size. It must be massive."

SAS Instructor: "Right...hang on there a minute..... I'm fucking coming with you!"

The SAS employed EX-US and New Zealand Vietnam War Veterans to come out to Malacca and talk to the SAS soldiers about their own experiences during the Vietnam War in the 1960's. The Veterans showed the SAS what signs and symbols the Vietcong used in the jungle during the Vietnam War. For instance, if there was a leaf on a tree with a twig stuck through it; that would indicate that there would be a mine on the trail in front of them, and it was buried within one meter of where they were standing. This was teaching the SAS students about remaining observant whilst out on patrol. US, NZ and Australian Veterans were used on all the SAS jungle Courses because they had all served out in Vietnam in Combat Roles. They had a wealth of information that they could pass onto the next SAS lads.

The Veterans often encouraged the SAS candidate soldiers to patrol in front of them and they then took them through the same route again after they'd finished their patrol. The Veterans would then point out the tell-tale signs of where they had just been patrolling and what obvious signs they had given away to the enemy on the trail they'd been patrolling. This part of the Course was all about moving silently on a 'Hard Routine.' The patrols were to follow a strict practice of not smoking, not cooking meals and not using toothpaste. They all had to use plastic mugs and maintained a noise routine similar to that of Trappist Monks who were pledged to a vow of silence.

The Course Candidates had to be up before first-light and all their kit silently packed away and ready to move before first light. The SAS soldiers would then sit on their Bergens and wait till half-light arrived before silently moving off into the jungle for about an hour. The SAS would then move off their route of march, eat a cold breakfast before packing up yet again, and then they would return back onto their original route of march. It was all aimed at throwing any enemy trackers off their trail.

George has previously worked with the famous Fijian SAS tracker, Sgt Talaiasi Labalaba BEM, who was killed at Mirbat Fort in Dhofar, on 19 July 1972. Labalaba was doing some tracking in a jungle one day and George was the number two in his Patrol. The details of why and where they were, and who they were tracking, still can't be divulged, even now.

Labalaba signalled to George that he was stopping to examine the trail. After observing the track for a few minutes, he picked up a leaf and scrutinised it before silently signalling that he knew their 'prey' had gone to the left, and that the patrol was going to follow them. Talaiasi Labalaba was the ultimate SAS tracker and if he were hunting someone down, it would be a sure bet that he'd definitely catch them unaware.

Another tracker, who served in the New Zealand (NZ) SAS, was Cpl Hughie Woods. Hughie was of Māori descent and had served in the Malayan jungle in 1956 where he hunted down Communist Terrorists (CT's). At least a couple of weeks before deploying into the jungle, Hughie stopped eating meat in his everyday diet, which he believed dramatically improved his sense of smell. Hughie had trained himself to detect other human-beings in the jungle by using the body odours of his adversaries to sniff them out.

Soldiers are taught about Shape, Shine, Shadow, and Noise that give away a soldiers presence in the field, smell is another element of detection that George Henderson also experienced in the jungle. He detected the smell of someone smoking tobacco in the jungle and yet they were more than two hundred meters away from where he was laid up, George silently signalled this fact to the others in his patrol, but they thought he was losing the plot because they couldn't smell anything.

The patrol continued on their hunt and George eventually heard a strange buzzing sound coming from somewhere out of the jungle. He again went to ground and tugged his earlobe to let the others in the patrol know that he had heard something.

Again, they thought George was losing his mind because they hadn't heard anything. Within another fifty meters, George found the enemy patrol they were hunting.

The SAS conducted an Exercise in the jungle against the Malaysian Army, whom George says are very courageous soldiers, but they are just as graceless and maladroit as most soldiers in any army. George has lost count of the times he'd heard Malaysian soldiers clanging their mess tins together, and shouting, "Fuck that hurt!" as they were either stung or bitten by some nasty jungle creature.

George, Labalaba, Cpl's Willie Wilson and Scouse Valelly SAS actually got into the middle of a Malaysian Army Jungle camp at night, totally undetected, by the soldiers camped there. The four-man SAS patrol caused mayhem in the bivouac area and ultimately had to do a bomb-burst (*Run off in different directions*) because they weren't sure what the Malayan soldiers would have done to them, had they actually been caught. But SAS soldiers are rarely caught by anyone tracking them because the SAS Jungle courses incorporated programs run by US, Australian and NZ veterans who had served during the Vietnam War. Up to that point, everything in British Military Jungle Warfare referred to the Malayan Emergency 1948-1960. All training had changed since that conflict though, and the Yank, Aussie and Kiwi armies were by then, generally more up to speed on Jungle Warfare, even more so than the British Army.

Soldiers around the world are, in the main, taught not to move after last light in the jungle. The problem for soldiers at night is you can't see your bloody hand in front of your face, the thick jungle canopy cutting out whatever meagre light is available at night. However, the SAS do move after dark in the jungle, but only to get to their next start point before first light. There is no way anyone can do any tracking at night in the jungle, but in today's modern army's, soldiers sometimes have up to date night vision goggles available.

Cpl Willie Wilson, who was in 24 Troop SAS, and the famous Labalaba were great friends and they had a private bet between the pair of them. The bet was for £1 and it involved either of them staying out of the UK for the longest period of time, be that because of operational tours or training courses. There is a way of manipulating tours and extending postings in the SAS, simply by making yourself available for training other soldiers - in particular, those from other foreign armies. Labalaba actually won the £1 bet in the end by constantly signing up to teaching Jungle Warfare Courses to the Aussie and NZ SAS Forces. Both of those superb warriors were to die in action, Labalaba at Mirbat Fort in Dhofar, and Willie who died in action working for the Sultan of Brunei.

When George and Scouse Valelly SAS had finished their Jungle Warfare training, they both flew to Singapore to pick up a flight to the UK and return to their SAS Headquarters in Hereford. Sadly, Scouse Valelly, who was a real ladies man and a superb jungle tracker, died in suspicious circumstances whilst on yet another SAS operational tour, this time in Italy.

Whilst on the Jungle Warfare Course, George had burned off a great deal of his excess body mass and after returning to Hereford, someone told him that he looked like a half-starved Gypsy's dog. Susie was used to George turning up a few stones lighter every-time he'd been away. She just accepted him looking thinner than a catwalk model whenever he came home. The two of them enjoyed a couple of weeks leave together before George had to report back for duty in Hereford.

George has done some amazing things during his time in the Special Forces, but he is restricted in what he can tell people in this book. Suffice it to say that some of his adventures have been included on certain television Programmes, *(Author's Note): Let's face it, everything the SAS does is TV and Media Gold*), but he still isn't at liberty to talk about them all.

Most avid readers of SAS books know that a vital skill of SAS soldiers is in being able to survive, live and fight in the extreme and harsh jungles of the world.

In his very younger days, Saturday morning matinees at the local Cinema, such as the Blythswood, Seemore and Roxy Cinemas on Maryhill Road and the Palace on Shawbridge Street, Pollokshaws for George was the main form of entertainment. Apart from cowboy westerns, he was particularly fond of the many war-films in the Far East jungle films that were often screened. As he got older, his fancy turned to library books on people/soldiers who had gone into the jungles of Malaya and Borneo to fight. Such as, 'The Jungle is Neutral.' by F Spencer-Chapman, or 'The War History of Tom Harrison (Borneo).' So, any fear he had of dark dangerous jungles was much diminished by the knowledge he'd found from reading and, when he got to the Far East, by visiting local museums in Singapore, Kuala Lumpur, and particularly the one set up by Tom

Harrison in Kuching. He had also met and spoken at length with a New Zealand SAS Veteran and expert jungle fighter called Hughie Woods.

So, George in the SAS, had already gained a limited experience of the jungle when he was with Air Despatch. In low work periods he managed to get himself attached to various units that had to go into the jungles of Malaya and Borneo for a few days at a time. He also did various jungle survival courses sponsored by the RAF, who ran the courses and were designed for RAF Pilots and Aircrew who might find themselves in survival situations should they have to ditch into the jungles or sea.
The SAS jungle training was a much longer, physically demanding and comprehensive course.

After the basic jungle training, his Tp was sent to a South American jungle country and after a couple of months, when George came out, once again he apparently looked like a Gypsy's dog, he was all skin and bones. George, even now is reluctant to and cannot speak much on this part of his Army service.

One thing he can talk about though, is when he went on his Norwegian language course. Because George was deploying on the NATO Northern flank in Norway, he needed to have the ability to converse with the locals in their own Norwegian tongue. (*Author's Note*): *Most intense army language Courses used to be conducted in the market town of*

Beaconsfield in Buckinghamshire, and many SAS soldiers went here before going out on Operation Storm to learn the Arabic language). George's Norwegian Course was held in Aldershot though, and it was taught by a Norwegian Education Corps Officer and one of the SAS wives, who just happened to be Norwegian herself.

George found Norwegian an easy language to learn because there were a lot of similarities to his own Scottish Native tongue. A child in Scotland is usually referred to as a 'bairn' and in Norway a child is called 'et barn' and there were plenty of other similarities between the two languages.

Unfortunately for George, there were two types of Norwegian language, Bokmal - which is Old Norwegian and Nynorsk which is New Norwegian. On his course, George was taught Nynorsk. George was going to spend the majority of his time on the Norway/Russian Northern Border where they only spoke old Norsk, so his communication with the locals was somewhat limited. However, when George went on his next SAS medic course to update his skills, he ended up in Casualty with a patient that no-one could understand. Someone found the patients driving licence, which turned out to be Norwegian, and George stepped up to translate everything for him and took all his details down. (*Author's Note*): *So, the language course wasn't a complete waste of Taxpayers money then George).*

It wasn't long before the SAS required George to learn other skills for yet another 'Job' and in this case this book can only tell you a small amount of information about his training and nothing about the 'Job.'

Royal Marines Snipers have been renown as being the best Marksmen in the world, from the early part of the last century right up to date. The RM standards of excellence in shooting is so exceptional that the SAS sent George off to them to learn how to be a sniper. George was sent on the 13-week Sniper Course down at the Royal Marines Training Centre (RMTC) at Lympstone, just south of Exeter.

George was still in G Sqn at the time of the Course and it was held after he'd returned from his part in the Dhofar war. The weapon the students trained on was the L42A1 which was used in the Dhofar War and Northern Ireland, but questionably saw its finest work carried out during the Falklands War in 1982. The L42A1 was not dissimilar to the British .303 bolt action Lee Enfield rifle of WW1 and WW2 fame.

The Royal Marines Sniper Course at Lympstone, which included a couple of Para Candidates. The 'Chunky' Sgt instructor in the front row 2nd from the right was very abrasive and didn't take to George until the final piss up at the end of the Course. The OIC, sitting next to him, was killed in a car accident not long after the course had finished. George is in the rear rank fourth from the left.

Work from the Course get-go involved a lot of judging distances and stalking the Sniper Instructors on Woodbury Common, (*Author's Note*): *George says he is still plucking thorns out of his arse today*). The candidates had to get within 100 -150 meters of the Instructors without being spotted. The Instructors were sitting on the high ground on a couple of G1098 canvas chairs and were searching the foreground using some high-powered binoculars.

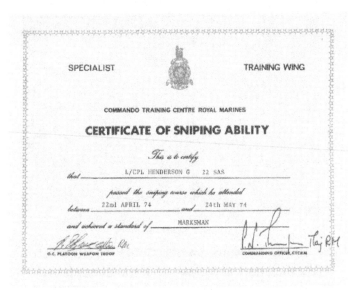

SPECIALIST   TRAINING WING

COMMANDO TRAINING CENTRE ROYAL MARINES

CERTIFICATE OF SNIPING ABILITY

This is to certify

that _____ L/CPL HENDERSON G   22 SAS _____

passed the sniping course which he attended

between _____ 22nd APRIL 74 _____ and _____ 24th MAY 74 _____

and achieved a standard of _____ MARKSMAN _____

O.C. PLATOON WEAPON TROOP   COMMANDING OFFICER, CTCRM

**George's end of Course Certificate
for the RM Sniper Course**

If they spotted someone using the dead ground properly but had exposed a piece of equipment or themselves, the Instructors would radio the soldiers patrolling the foreground and talk them onto the exact point where they spotted the approaching sniper. Each student was allowed to be spotted only once and after that they would be binned off the Course. George was spotted only once during the entire Course.

SPECIALIST   TRAINING WING

COMMANDO TRAINING CENTRE ROYAL MARINES

CERTIFICATE OF SNIPING ABILITY

This is to certify
that _GEORGE HENDERSON (ANGO)_

passed the sniping course which he attended
between _THEN_ and _NOW_

and achieved a standard of _RUBBISH_

O.C. PLATOON WEAPON TROOP   COMMANDING OFFICER, CTCRM

George's other end of Course Certificate for the RM Sniper Course. This only goes to prove that Royal Marine Commandos, 'do' have a minimal and 'rubbish' sense of humour.

One night during the Course, George was waiting in the queue by the pay telephones in the NAAFI foyer and he overheard a RM recruit speaking to his Mum on one of the phones. "I'm sick to death of this Mum, the Instructors are badgering us 24 hours a day and whatever we do isn't good enough for them. They keep picking on us all the time. I'm thinking of leaving the Royal Marines and trying out for that SAS lot." George thought to himself, 'Good luck with that mate'.

CHAPTER EIGHT

DUISBURG HERE I COME!

At the end of George's time in the SAS he was on the list for promotion to Warrant Officer Class 2 (WO2). He initially went back to the RCT Depot in Buller Barracks as a Sgt where he was a Weapons Instructor in the Depots Skill At Arms Training Wing. He taught weapon handling to recruits and also on the Senior and Junior Drill Courses.

This was an essential transition into the real world of the British Army for George. He had to calm down from how things were done in the Special Forces. He could no longer simply step on someone's neck just to get things achieved and now had to observe some of the niceties of military life and join the real world of the British Army. This was a great military leveller for George and it prepped his transition back into normal Army life.

George definitely did not want to go to a transport unit in BAOR, Germany but it was inevitable that he accepted whatever he was 'offered', which turned out to be 35 Sqn RCT within 3 ADTR RCT in Duisburg, West Germany.

George was eventually promoted to SSgt within the RCT Depot and placed in one of the RCT Training

Troops. George was eventually promoted to WO2 before being posted to 3 Armoured Division Transport Regiment RCT (3 ADTR RCT) in Duisburg, where he was to take over as 35 Sqn's Sergeant Major (SSM). He'd previously written to his new CO, OC, RSM and even to the Sgt's Mess Manager in Duisburg, giving them his flight details and telling them when he would be arriving at the unit. He also wrote to the Sgt's Mess Manager informing him that he would need a room in the Sgt's Mess because he'd initially be unaccompanied on the posting. George would eventually be allocated a Married Quarter in Duisburg so that Susie could visit and stay with him for short visits.

When George arrived at Dusseldorf Airport, he had to get a taxi to the camp in Duisburg because there wasn't any transport to meet him, despite all his letters to 3 ADTR's key personnel. (_Author's Note_): _Unfortunately, George was in for a bit of a surprise, because the whole of 3 ADTR had deployed out into the field on Exercise and there was only minimal personnel in the camp on duty._) He got out of the cab when the Mercedes Taxi pulled up outside the camp gates and the Driver Sentry on the gate nonchalantly came over towards him and said,

Sentry: "Yeah, what can I do for you mate?"

George: "I'm just joining the unit. Tell me, where's the Sgt's Mess?"

Sentry: "Everyone is on Exercise mate, don't think anyone's there."

Ignoring the soldier, who was obviously only in possession of a couple of braincells, George headed over to the Sgt's Mess and spoke to the bloke who was standing in for the Mess Manager whilst the Regt was out on Exercise.

Mess Manager: "Didn't know you were coming, mate."

George: "Even though I wrote to the Mess Manager giving him my arrival date and timings?"

Mess Manager: "I don't know anything about that mate? Tell you what though, you can use the Duty Bunk if you like?"

The Duty Bunk was, in the words of a very annoyed WO2 George Henderson RCT, "Fucking Honking." The bedding hadn't been changed or laundered and there weren't even any clean sheets he could put on the bed. There was no way he was going to sleep in a filthy bunk for a week, so he said to the Pay

Warrant Officer, "I'm off back to England. When the Regt wants me, call me at home." He made his way back to the Airport and flew back to Gatwick and then took a train to his house in Brighton where he stayed for a couple of weeks. There wasn't any backlash from this because he'd simply decided to go back to the UK, on his own authority.

A few days later he received a call saying the Sqn wanted to see him. Without giving any flight details, George made his way back to Duisburg, booked in the Mess and told the Mess Manager to ring 35 Sqn and tell them he was here. He then changed into uniform and made his way into the HQ building where the Regimental Sergeant Major, WO 1 (RSM) John Rayer (RCT) took him to see the Commanding Officer (CO). Nothing was said about his initial brief arrival and immediate departure back to the UK! George was technically at fault, as when soldiers are posted it comes in the form of a 'Posting Order' but under the circumstances, George had decided that it would be best to keep silent on this oversight!

The CO was a very respected and genuinely nice man, but his message was clear. George was to use his big stick (pace stick) and get things in the Sqn sorted. After this interview the message was made even plainer by the RSM.

The CO explained that 35 Sqn was a recently re-formed Sqn. It was made up from a lot of officers, senior and junior NCO's and Drivers that other RCT units had sent to them, so that a brand-new 35 Sqn RCT could be reformed. George is unequivocal about the sort of men 'some' other units had sent to the new Sqn. He told me, "If you were an SSM somewhere in BAOR and you had one of the following in your Sqn - a crap Driver, a thief, a violent bully or a border-line alcoholic, *(Author's Note): Let's face it, the majority of service personnel in BAOR at that time during the Cold War were all borderline alkies)* and you suddenly receive a signal telling you to send any surplus soldiers to 35 Sqn, who are you going to choose to send?" George continued, "Don't get me wrong, there were some extremely good Drivers and NCO's sent to 35 Sqn, but they also received their fair share of dross from other units. Some of the despatching SSM's were probably thinking, 'It's a shame I can't send another six as well.'

The CO warned George that some of the soldiers within his new Sqn would need an influx of harsh discipline from their new SSM, and that included officers as well as NCO's and Drivers. The CO, a Lt Col, went on, "Sarn't Major, you have cart-blanche and my absolute authority to do whatever is necessary to bring this Sqn in to line."

George didn't discuss with his new CO about this being his first ever posting to a Div Tp Regt, and that this was his first ever appointment as an SSM. Remember, George was trying to adopt a new and different philosophy to the one he was used to in the SAS. (_Author's Note_): _Bear in mind dear reader, a philosophy of life is an overall vision and interpretation of the purpose or attitude toward our own existence_).

A Senior NCO for 35 Sqn was waiting outside the RSMs office to take George to the Sqn HQ. On arrival at the SSM's office George was surprised to see how relaxed it was with fishing rods and kit lying around. The outgoing SSM asked if he wanted a coffee, 'Yes' George replied. The SSM called a driver in and using the drivers first name said get two coffees. George thought, "I've got a lot to learn about life in a Div Regt!"

Next was the Officer Commanding's(OC's) interview, which went rather well. The OC was a Scotsman with a great sense of humour and tremendous life experience. Prior to enlistment he had worked in the diamond mines in South Africa and in senior management in various well known technical companies. He did not offer George any direction but George felt comfortable in his task ahead. He knew that he would not be a popular 'nice guy' as he felt he had a job to do in this recently reformed Sqn. He reflected on his own experiences when he was a young soldier and had, as with others, held the Sergeant Major as being an awesome, terrifying person, but one who held the admiration of all as the epitome of justice and discipline in the units. He was always the best turned out and some he knew, wore a fresh, ironed shirt every morning and changed into another for the afternoon. In essence, from what he had just experienced, the Sqn needed a traditional Sergeant Major in the manner that he had watched great Sergeant Majors using their particular management skills in the very varied units he had served (SAS, Para, Infantry and of course his own Corps). He knew he was being watched by those youngsters who would progress through the ranks to eventually do his job, as indeed he himself had done.

George Henderson gave the author his philosophy of military life within an RCT unit, "As soon as you get rid of one wanker, you'll soon get another one to take his place." George believes that you are better off leaving things as they are and use what you've been given; he believes you can change some of the men under your command by simply training and inspiring them to become better soldiers. The Sqn had had a few SSM's before George had arrived and they weren't particularly bothered about improving the prestige and status of the Sqn, for 'whatever' various reasons.

George targeted the most senior of his Senior NCO's, the Troop Staff Sgt's. He told them he was going to come down hard on everyone in the Sqn, including officers, with his big stick. Rather than being upset by his declaration, the Tp Staffies said, "Thank fuck for that, Sir! If we had sent anyone over to our previous SSM's for disciplinary matters, they were usually dealt with by kid gloves, given a nice cup of tea and given a kind word in their ear." Things were about to change radically within 35 Sqn RCT.

One Driver in 35 Sqn had been given a nasty beating by a couple of bullies in the accommodation block during the night. This had been a couple of months before George had arrived at Duisburg and the young Driver had to be hospitalised as a result of the going over. George found out who had done the dirty deed and collared one of the bullies in the gymnasium while the nasty piece of work was doing some bag work whilst boxing training. George squared up to this particularly nasty tyrant and offered him the chance to go head-to-head with him for a couple of rounds in the boxing ring. The bully turned George down flat, "No way sir, if I put you down on the canvas you will put me in jail." George snarled at the bully and whispered in his ear, "What makes you think you'll get the chance to fucking lay a glove on me boy?"

George laid the law down in no uncertain terms and told him to put the news out to the other bullies of what was going to happen to them if they ever stepped out of line again. As their SSM, George found that the 'Tough Guys' within the Sqn just needed some guidance, because when they found out that there was an even tougher guy in the Sqn, they automatically fell into line and became good soldiers. One of the bullies eventually went on to become a conscientious and very good RSM. Word soon got around 3 ADTR about the SSM from 35 Sqn, as the following anecdote will reflect.

At Christmas time, George went out into the German countryside with a Land Rover and a saw. He cut down a couple of decent German Christmas trees and brought them back to camp, one for himself and the other for the Sqn HQ. The RSM saw George driving back into camp with the trees strapped onto the top of his Land Rover. The RSM then had the following telephone conversation with the Guardroom's Regimental Police (RP) Corporal.

RSM: "Provost! I want you to phone all the SSM's and tell them to be in my office in the next half an hour."

Provost Cpl: "No problem sir, as it happens the SSM of 35 Sqn has just come back into camp."

RSM: "I know, and he's got a couple of Christmas trees strapped onto his Land Rover."

Provost Cpl: "Yes I know he has Sir. I've just seen them."

RSM: "Well, while the SSM's are heading up to my office, I want you to steal one of those Christmas trees off his Land Rover and put it to one side for me. But keep quiet about it though."

Provost Cpl: ""You do know that those Christmas trees belong to SSM Henderson don't you, Sir?"

RSM: "So?"

Provost Cpl: "Well, I'm afraid I can't steal one of those trees off his Land Rover, Sir."

RSM: "Why not, Corporal?"

Provost Cpl: "Sarn't Major Henderson served in the Special Air Service Sir. He is hard as nails and is known within 3 ADTR as GBH (*Grievous Bodily Harm*), and I would rather cross you than some-one everyone in the unit calls, George Bastard Henderson."

The RSM never did get one of those particular Christmas trees that he'd wanted to be nicked off George's Land Rover.

Whilst he was the SSM at 35 Sqn, George believed that all soldiers were actors and that each soldier had a particular character performance to portray, every single day. George had been assigned the character part of a British Army Sergeant Major to play in his latest role. Most people see that as a particularly fearsome part, and so that was how he 'acted' in the part. George thought to himself, 'If I act like that in my role, hopefully everyone will believe it and the discipline within the unit will be corrected'.

He told the author on interview, "Harry, all I had to do was look mean and moody whilst carrying a big stick. Everyone would then be terrified of me and behave themselves accordingly. I'm not generally a violent man Harry, but I can certainly look the part."

Anyway, it worked very well in this case and discipline within 35 Sqn improved dramatically, George's fine acting certainly paid off. *(Author's Note): From what the author has heard about George's acting abilities from ex members of 35 Sqn RCT, George Henderson must have Laurence Olivier'd his arse off in the role of 'The Scary Sergeant Major.' For George's theatrical performance he should have been presented with at least an Academy Award, an Emmy, a Screen Actors Guild Award and four fucking Tony Awards at least. Just saying!"*

Whilst maintaining discipline within 35 Sqn, George travelled home to see Susie on every weekend that he could get away from the unit and back to the UK. He was lucky in that he received cheap flights because Suzie was an airline pilot with KLM and he flew home as often as time, duties, flights and Exercises allowed. At close of play on a Friday afternoon, George would drive round to Dusseldorf airport whilst loosening his boot laces and taking off his Heavy Duty Jumper. In the staff car park he'd whip off his shirt, Jumper, trousers, army socks and replace them with his own civilian clothes. George had several spare uniforms in Duisburg and he'd rotate their use so he wouldn't have to faff around during the weekend getting them ready for the next weeks 'Olivier Awards.' He'd climb over the security fence and drop down into the airport grounds before running off towards the Departures Lounge. *(Author's Note): This reads something like a James Bond novel).*

He always had his passport and flight documents available at short notice and everyone on the KLM Staff knew George because he was married to Suzie. There was one occasion on a Friday when he arrived late at Departures and he was told the KLM Gate was already closing. He was told, "You'd better hurry, George, they are about to close the gate. You're going to have to sprint if you want to get on board the plane!" George ran as fast as he could to the gate and found the aircraft door was already closed and so he rapped on the window; one of the aircrew looked through the window and said, "Oh, hiya George, hang on a minute, I'll open the door for you". *(Author's Note): What a privileged life style you used to lead George).* Every passenger on the aircraft was staring quizzically at George after he sat down on his seat, desperately trying to get his breath back.

In all, George served just over five years with the SAS. He had an offer of becoming Permanent Cadre. This meant that he would be transferred from the RCT Manning and Records to the Infantry and would remain in Hereford for the rest of his time in the Army. Big decision, but he had completed a major ambition, that was to be a member of the SAS for three years and had now done five years. He had also wanted to find out what it was like to be in a battle, he had now done that many times and was content with his performance.

After serving in the SAS, it was decision time - leave the Army or serve on. As he was happy in Aldershot and felt that it was his second home, and although he would have preferred to go back to 63 Para Sqn, sadly the Defence Review decimated the old life there, so RCT Manning and Records decided to post him to Depot RCT in the rank of Sergeant.

On arrival in Buller, he was sent to the Skill at Arms Wing as a Weapon Training Instructor, where he taught on the NCO Promotion courses. After a few months he was moved from the training wing on promotion to 64 Sqn RCT, as a Tp Staff Sgt. This was extremely educational for George as he had only been in Corps Specialised Units and so felt he needed to carefully rethink his attitude towards the modern young men who were joining the Army and also to reflect on how young and immature he was when he'd made the journey to Bordon.

Although George enjoyed various sports, and played rugby as one of the Depot's Regimental Team, the one activity that had taken him over, was Freefall

Parachuting. He had been doing this for some years now and most weekends travelled to the Army Parachute Centre at Netheravon, where the Freefall Parachute jumps were cheaper than the civilian clubs.

Free Fall Sport Parachuting is not just a case of jumping from a plane, opening the parachute and dropping to the ground. Netheravon was therefore a good place to learn and develop the skills to compete in style and accuracy competitions.

Style is where a set sequence of body manoeuvres were given to the free fallers, such as, timed body turns and back and forward loops. Points were given for accurate turns and loops. There was also accuracy where the parachutist, when under the canopy, aimed for a gravel pit with a target disc in the centre of the pit with his/her foot. There was also link ups. This is where the parachutists exit the aircraft and link up in various formations with other parachutists in mid-air.

As there were a few Corps sport parachutists in the Aldershot area, Lt Col (then Maj) Tom Ridgeway, called a meeting in Buller Barracks for all Corps Free Fallers. Tom Ridgeway was an ex-Air Despatcher and OC of 63 Para Sqn and an experienced Free Fall Parachuter himself. About 14 turned up at the meeting where the main point was the feasibility of setting up a Corps Free Fall Display Team.

Many of the Corps Jumpers were 'bandits,' a loose term for unaffiliated Free Fallers who parachuted into displays with full recognised Free Fall Teams. Those included were, the Parachute Regt's ' Red Devils' (also known as the 'Freds') and the Royal Artillery's 'Black Nights.'. Those attending the meeting agreed that there was now enough Free Fallers to set up a Corps Free Fall Team, who were willing to give their free time in support. Like all teams they needed a name. Many were suggested, but the one fielded by (the then) Maj 'Ozzy' Osborne was the obvious choice, 'The Silver Stars.' Think Cap Badge, 'an eight pointed replica of the Star of India!' Parachute displays started to take place every weekend in Summer.

The 'Freds' and the other major display parachute team in Aldershot area, The Royal Artillery Display Team, had full diaries. So, to capitalise, the 'Silver Stars' began to take bookings for paying events within the civilian communities. Initially, George and other team members drove around the county area looking at village posters to get details of fetes. Then they called the fete organisers to offer a Free Fall Parachute display into their event. This was moderately successful in establishing the display team and gaining funds. The 'Silver Stars,' were, of course, popular at RCT Corps events, although no monies were charged, other than the cost of the Aircraft flying time. However, cash raised from the civilian displays helped buy new rigs (parachutes) with canopies in Corps colours.

George

CHAPTER NINE

DUISBURG AND NORTHERN IRELAND

When George arrived at 35 Sqn, the unit (3 ADTR) was due to depart for an operational tour in Northern Ireland. George was acting RSM of 3 ADTR for the entire tour because the RSM of the Regt couldn't serve out in Ulster because he was a Northern Irishman by birth and he would have been a target for all factions of terrorist groups in the country. George filled in as RSM and he handled all of the soldiers of 3 ADTR who deployed out to Moscow Camp, Belfast. They were a mixed bunch that were made up of numerous different RCT units based in BAOR, including some from 10 Regt RCT who'd volunteered to go with 3 ADTR.

The Northern Ireland Training went exceptionally well and on arrival in theatre, sections were dispersed to the various units around Belfast. George oversaw everything, nothing escaped his attention and apart from one bad incident, the Sqn was extremely successful. Northern Ireland was classed as a 'Corporals War' and when in Northern Ireland, George had visited the many different locations, and he was impressed by the performance of all the section commanders and soldiers and the fantastic relationships they had formed with the host units they were supporting.

Weapon Training was something that George was particularly enthusiastic about. He'd been through the Borneo Campaign, P Coy, the hostile withdrawal from Aden, he'd been a Weapons Instructor at the RCT Depot, and he'd also been through SAS Selection and had served in the SAS during the Dhofar War. The one thing that George wasn't going to take lightly was Weapon Handling. Para and SAS training had taught him that at the very least - but you can't allow for every soldier and every circumstance.

The soldiers deploying out to Ulster with 3 ADTR came from various RCT units because every Operation Banner ('OP BANNER') Tour was always the same. During the Cold War, every unit was supplemented by soldiers who wore the same sort of cap badge. The Royal Green Jackets, Parachute Regiment, Queens Regiment and every cap badge in the British Army were always short of soldiers for Northern Ireland Tours. George seems to recall RCT soldiers coming to 3 ADTR from larger RCT units like 10 Regiment RCT in Bielefeld, because the bigger the unit, the more soldiers they had to spare. When 3 ADTR did their Northern Ireland Training it was carried out in Glamorgan Barracks with the Driver

Training being conducted on the local German roads.

A Northern Ireland Tactics and Training Advisory Team (NITAT) crew came down to Duisburg and helped George and his teams out with their training schedules. (*Author's Note*): *When this author did his first tour of Northern Ireland in 1976, a NITAT team came from Sennelager to 10 Regt RCT in Bielefeld and gave some fantastic lectures on a multitude of subjects about Northern Ireland. The team had some really switched-on soldiers from the Royal Army Ordnance Corps (RAOC), Small Arms School Corps (SASC) and also from the Intelligence Corps. The following is a brief excerpt about the sort of things that NITAT did for units deploying out to Ulster and is taken from my book 'Harry was a Crap Hat' - Second Edition).*

'The Warrant Officer introduced himself and his team before explaining that they were there to give us an insight to the current situation in NI and hopefully give us enough advice to help us make it through our four-month tour, unscathed. He then asked if anyone in the audience could pick up any weapon on the table and identify it by name and calibre. I (Harry Clacy) noticed a US .303 Garand on the table and so I stuck my hand up. "Good!" said the WO 2, "Step forward and pick up the one you've recognised and give a 30 second talk on everything you know about that particular

weapon." I started to wrack my brains about anything I could remember about the Garand, like which wars it had been used in, I wanted to impress the instructors and my peers. As I picked up the rifle and turned towards everyone in the cinema, a loud explosion detonated behind me, my ears were ringing and I coughed in my combat trousers. The explosion was so loud that it made everyone in the cinema jump and they probably also coughed in their combat trousers.

By the fire exit, a short distance from the stage, was a biscuit tin and its lid had been blown off as I picked up the rifle, the NITAT team had to open the fire doors to clear the dense smoke. That was my first and last booby trap; the sound of my RCT mates laughing at my entrapment made my humiliation even harder to bear'.

Meanwhile back to the 3 ADTR RCT tour of Belfast, it was progressing very well, right up until a small mobile Armoured Personnel Carrier (APC) patrol pulled up next to a telephone box on the street. A Royal Pioneer Corps (RPC) soldier from the patrol wanted to telephone his girlfriend back in Germany, the phone call would only be of a short duration and the patrol could then continue with their perambulations without causing any sort of kerfuffle. In the back of the patrol vehicle, one of the other soldiers was fiddling with the safety catch on his weapon, (a weapon that had already been cocked and had a round up the spout). It had been cocked and was ready to fire.

The rifle suddenly jumped in the soldiers hand and a deafening noise reverberated inside the back of the APC,. The troop-carrying area was suddenly filled with the smell of cordite.

The young RPC soldier was in the way of that discharged bullet and he was killed immediately. Not intentionally, but killed none the less by what the British Army term as a 'Negligent Discharge.' Those sort of incidents happen when soldiers are using live ammunition on Operational Tours and they start to lose their concentration because of tiredness, boredom, or just plain old bad soldiering. That excuse doesn't help the soldier who has just had his brains blown out though. There, but for the grace of good/bad luck, goes many a soldier.

When George was posted away from 35 Sqn RCT he was presented with a crystal decanter on the steps that led into the Sqn HQ. Although he's never been keen on senior ranks receiving gifts when leaving a unit, George had no choice but to accept it because it had already been bought for him. "I simply did my job as it was asked of me. Soldiers shouldn't be bought gifts for basically doing what they were paid to do. In some units I've served in, the NCO's put in what amounted to a shopping list when they were leaving. The list included sizes, colours and particular designs of the items they wanted to receive. It's supposed to be a gift from friends, so you shouldn't demand the particular gift that you want and think you deserve".

After returning to Duisburg, the unit had leave, then life returned to normal BAOR routine.

Susie had flown over to Duisburg for George's leaving function with the intention of driving back to the UK with him in his sporty MG BGT. George had previously bought the car off a real character called WO1 Steven Loseby. The small car was stuffed to the gunnels with suitcases containing all of George's uniforms, and it was difficult to find any spare space for the gift Decanter.

On arrival at Dover Ferry Port, the Customs Officials made George empty the entire car so they could check he wasn't trying to smuggle any extra fags or bottles of booze into the UK. It was galling for George because the paradox was that he and Susie didn't have anything they weren't entitled to carry, but as George says, "They were just doing their job. They simply see squaddies returning to the UK with plenty of Duty-Free goods and think they are all going to try and smuggle a few extra bits and pieces past the customs."

George and Susie had to re-load the car with the entire contents of their car that was stacked up at the side of the road. (*Author's Note*): *Perhaps you both looked very suspicious*).

George was selected for promotion to Warrant Officer Class 1 (WO1), and was posted to the Headquarters, Allied Command Europe (ACE) Mobile Force in Bulford as Regimental Sergeant Major (RSM). This involved working closely with other NATO forces on joint exercises.

CHAPTER TEN

AN OFFICER AND GENTLEMAN

After 18 months with the ACE Mobile Force, George was selected for a Commission. Following what was known as the 'Knife and Fork' course at the Officers' Mess in Buller Barracks, Aldershot, he was sent to 19 Infantry and Signal Squadron in Colchester as the Motor Transport Officer (MTO). This involved the unit going to Germany in support of Divisional Exercises. Due to a regrading of this post, he was, after nine months, posted again. His replacement was Angus Paterson, who George had served with in Bulford when Angus was with the Tank Transporter Unit there.

George's next appointment was as Officer Commanding, 414 Tank Transporter Unit in Bulford. As the title indicates, it involved transporting tanks belonging to the UK based Tank Regiment and other heavy equipment around the UK using the mighty Antar Transporter. However, shortly after taking up this post, the unit started to receive the new 'Commander' Tank Transporter and the Trailers, that were designed to carry the new Challenger Tanks. 414 was the first unit to be issued with this powerful and super rig. A majority of the unit action was collecting the new 'Challengers' from the factory and delivering them to Southampton docks for onward transmission to BAOR.

George with the 'Mighty Antar'

George and Capt Bob Ferguson with the Crusader

414 was often tasked to pick up and convey many other varied types of equipment for delivery throughout the UK and the unit was mindful to ensure it did not transport anything that exceeded the trailer design weight. Quite often George demanded written confirmation of the weight of loads, to ensure it did not exceed the design weight carriage limit of the trailers (65 tonnes) as they were constructed with pre stressed tensile steel. Some tank hulks that were being used as targets on live firing ranges, that needed to be moved, were filled with concrete and estimated to weigh over a hundred tonnes!

Tank Transporters are deemed 'Indivisible Loads' and therefore their movement throughout the UK meant that every council, electricity and waterwork companies, also Police Authorities en route, had to be notified. Recces had to be done to ensure routes and roads were suitable. Old, recognised routes constantly changed with new road networks and motorways being built. Driving hours as per UK law were, of course, strictly observed.

The Ops Room was manned 24 hours a day to support the crews, who were required to stay with the vehicles, sometimes for days, until the task was completed. There was never any shortage of willing drivers for those long journeys and George had a busy time signing claim forms for these hard working, specialised drivers. Within the Corps, the

Tank Transporter Crews were classified as A grade which meant a higher pay band. When George was a driver, he was in the usual B pay scale. Many Tank Transporter drivers preferred to remain within the Tank Transporter trade, spending many years in one unit but yo-yo'ing between the UK and the BAOR Tank Transporter Units. It stands that quite a few of the wives were German. By choosing to stay in Tank Transporting this might have inadvertently affected some individual's promotion, as George found quite a few long in the tooth Tank Transporter Drivers in various ranks in the unit.

Shortly after coming into 414, George visited the workshops and counted about 20 soldiers in overalls busily working on the vehicles. He mentioned to the workshop boss, the Artificer Sergeant Major (ASM), that he seemed to have more mechanics than the establishment chart showed. The ASM replied that many of the drivers had been with Tank Transporting for so long, they had great knowledge of the Antar vehicle mechanics and he was happy for them to do certain repairs but that all jobs were checked and signed off on the repair sheet by his Workshop Manager. George realised this was a gift, as many regarded the ageing Antar's as being a breakdown waiting to happen.

Often spare parts were difficult to get. Against all procedures, an Antar with a serious defect awaiting major repair, found itself being 'cannibalised' to keep others on the road!

Thankfully, the motivation of the workshop and crews was excellent and although the overall availability of 22 Rigs for operation percentage was not good due to the age of the vehicles, there was always enough to legally meet the daily tasks. As per all soldier/drivers, they preferred to be out of camp on the road, rather than the dull routine of being in basecamp.

After being commissioned for just 18 months and posted to 414 from 19 Bde, (due to change of posting rank, e.g. from Captain to WO1). It was no cushy posting!

Change was everywhere in the MOD. The 'threat' of defence cuts, always hanging overhead. Financial awareness was reaching ever downwards and George found that he was to be gifted with the first 'Unit Executive Responsibility Budget' in the Army. George had an additional task of working to a budget on top of receiving the new Scammell Commander into service, which was replacing the ageing Antar.

The accountants moved in and everything was being costed. As a first stage, much time was 'spent' on producing basic costings from manpower to equipment and real estate. It was agreed that a comparison (of sorts) would be used against a civilian transport company doing as close as possible, the same load tasks. It worked out that a transport company could move a tank with overall costs much less than they could at 414 Tk Tptr Tp. George realised that with the trend for civilianisation of Military work, the UK Tank Transport Unit could be considered obsolete. So, much 'in-house' scrutiny had to be taken into consideration to somehow reduce costs. He also had to think of soldier retention at a time when there was lower recruiting. Most of these experienced drivers could leave the Army and get a similar job with more money with a civilian firm. Nevertheless, he had no option other than to start cost cutting as quickly but as delicately as possible, without hitting the soldiers pay packets too much. At his handover (leaving the unit), costs had been reduced, but the accountant was in the door and much further cuts would have to be made.

By this time, George had reached his end of tour and was posted to 20 Sqn RCT in Regents Park Barracks, London, as the Admin Officer (AO). He reflected on that day many years before when the Careers Officer in Depot RASC told him he was going to be a clerk, and wondered if he had now made a serious mistake!

After a couple of months, the OC, Peter Harpur, spoke to George and said he had just had a call from

PB8, (the MOD office that dealt with officer matters). George was told that a sudden vacancy had come up in 56 Sqn RCT in Woolwich and would he go there as OC. Within a couple of days, he was there and getting familiar with his new job. The Sqn's task was to provide administrative transport support to the Garrison HQ, Depot RA and Woolwich Hospital. There were three Troops. One was manned by RA drivers, a Troop of mixed WRAC and RCT drivers and a third Troop of civilian drivers.

Although a major task of 56 Sqn RCT was to support the Depot RA's Recruit Training Batteries transport needs, it was under equipped for Troop/Load Carrying Vehicles. They relied heavily on the goodwill and support of London Territorial Batteries by borrowing their 4 Tonne vehicles to support the Recruit Batteries in their basic Field Training Exercises. The goodwill from the TA was outstanding, as was the hard-working RA Tp SSgt who spent many hours calling round the various TA units to beg/borrow and collect their vehicles. It worked extremely well but George had 'Plan B' in waiting, the RLC TA Sqn's!

56 Sqn also held on charge a fleet of Ambulances that were there to fulfil an emergency plan in the event of major conflict. These vehicles, technically, belonged to the Royal Army Medical Corps (RAMC) but it made absolute sense for the Tpt Sqn to hold and maintain them. Within this fleet was an ancient

bull-nosed out of date Ambulance that if ever this fleet was used, would be the last out of the gates.

As always, Defence Cuts appeared and George, along with all other similar Unit Commanders, had to select and justify a 20% reduction in vehicle holdings. This was not easy, as the job/role of every vehicle had to be scrutinised. The effect of a 20% loss never seemed to be an argument for units by the Reviewing Committees.

George will not forget the day when he faced the Review Committee. It was chaired by someone George had met before in the Logistic Support Battalion when he was Major Ironside (now Lt Colonel) RAOC. Past experience told George that this man would see through any waffle or flam immediately. Also, that the Committee could override the offerings submitted by units. George stood by for a hard time and hoped that he would not have to suffer too much from an alternative loss of vehicles.

In his turn with other Sqn/unit representatives, he entered the room ready to be interrogated on his offering. The chairing Colonel looked at it in front of him, then said "OK, so for your 20% cut you want to offer up a 30-year-old ambulance that isn't even yours?" As George knew, the Colonel had done his research!

How could you answer that? To his surprise it was accepted and George left the interview feeling his analysis of the Sqn holdings with justifications must have touched the spot! It was nevertheless with sadness that this old relic was going to Military sales and would probably be sold off at auction for a minimal amount.

Chatting to other Unit Commanders after the interviews, many felt they had been mugged, as they came out having lost more than they had offered!

George's next appointment was to the Royal Military Academy Sandhurst (RMAS) as 2i/c of HQ Wing. It was not what George wanted, but he tried it before making up his mind. The job basically had a board with hundreds of names on it. His job was to ensure by liaison with all the Manning and Records Offices, that when someone was posted, a suitable replacement was specially selected as this was a high profile establishment.

This appointment confirmed his reservations and thoughts and he made his mind up that he was going to resign. He duly wrote to PB8 offering, with regret, his resignation. George started to plot the way ahead for work beyond the Army with great excitement, but with some trepidation, as the Army had been his life since he was 17 years old.

Following several phone calls, from 'Ted' in PB8, George was enticed to withdraw his resignation by the offer of a post at Shorncliffe, Folkestone, as OC 43 Transport and Movements Squadron RCT (43 Tpt & Mov Sqn RCT).

43 Tpt & Mov Sqn RCT was responsible for all transport and movements matters in Kent and East Sussex. In effect all units east of the A23, the London to Brighton main road. The Sqn also supported HQ 2 Infantry Brigade and the units based in Folkestone and Dover.

There was also a Movements Section, that dealt with all movement matters involving the resident and Territorial Units. Also, military personnel and their dependants travelling through the busy ports en route to/from BAOR.

As some of the civilian staff had family members working for the Channel Tunnel, George found himself with a 'friends of the tunnel' card that allowed him to cross at a reduced fare. It was such a pleasure to use the tunnel, do some shopping, have a meal in France, then return to Folkestone.

All in all it was, at most times, a dream posting with moments of high drama, but to serve in such a wonderful area was a gem. The only drawback was that after he had been there a couple of months, posting orders started to arrive for vehicles. The loss of some of them would require a lot of problem solving. It was poetic justice he supposed, as the losses were resulting from the vehicle holding review! His replacement at Woolwich, would not have that problem!

From there George had other postings, but preferred to stay in the UK, especially as there was going to be a withdrawal of troops from BAOR back to the UK and he did not particularly like Germany, feelings garnered from a few trips to various units over there.

He finished his Army service after he'd returned to Folkestone to Command 43 Tpt & Mov Sqn RCT for a second time. After that, he worked in the USA for some years, before returning to the UK and retiring to Essex, where he has since remained.

George's Medals from left to right:

MBE, GSM 1947 with Bar for Brunei (this medal was discontinued in 1962 and was replaced by the GSM 1962); GSM 1962 with Bars for Borneo, Malay Peninsula, South Arabia (Aden), Northern Ireland, Dhofar; Pingat Jasu Malaysia Medal for service on the mainland of Malaya during the Emergency; LS&GC (Long Service and Good Conduct) Medal.

Note: The Mentioned in Despatches Oak Leaf on the ribbon of the GSM 1962 was awarded for something George had done on an operational tour, but he isn't at liberty to explain.

Other books by Brian (Harry) Clacy

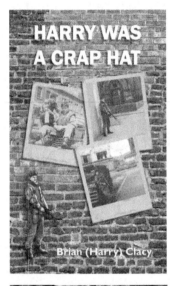

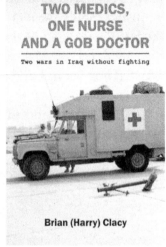

SOLDIERS
ON WHEELS

Drivers of the
RASC, RCT & RLC

Brian (Harry) Clacy

always
HARRY ʌ WAS
A CRAP HAT

Brian (Harry) Clacy

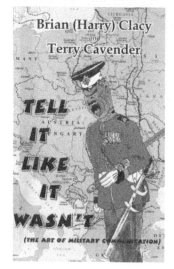

Brian (Harry) Clacy
Terry Cavender

TELL
IT
LIKE
IT
WASN'T

(THE ART OF MILITARY COMMUNICATION)

TELL IT LIKE IT WASN'T! (PART 2)
(The Art of Military Communication)

Brian (Harry) Clacy & Terry Cavender

FRANK'S WAR IN A
THORNEYCROFT

AN ARMY SERVICE CORPS DIARY
by Brian (Harry) Clacy

TRUCKS
AND
TROGS

Officers and Soldiers of the
Royal Corps of Transport

Brian (Harry) Clacy

Printed in Great Britain
by Amazon